First World War

and Army of Occupation

War Diary

France, Belgium and Germany

7 INDIAN (MEERUT) DIVISION
19 (Dehra Dun) Indian Infantry Brigade
Seaforth Highlanders
(Ross-shire Buffs, the Duke of Albany's)
4th Battalion.
2 November 1914 - 31 December 1915

WO95/3941/2

The Naval & Military Press Ltd
www.nmarchive.com
Published in association with The National Archives

Published by

The Naval & Military Press Ltd

Unit 10 Ridgewood Industrial Park,

Uckfield, East Sussex,

TN22 5QE England

Tel: +44 (0) 1825 749494

www.naval-military-press.com

www.nmarchive.com

This diary has been reprinted in facsimile from the original. Any imperfections are inevitably reproduced and the quality may fall short of modern type and cartographic standards.

Contents

Document type	Place/Title	Date From	Date To
Heading	WO95/3941/2 4 Battalion Seaforth Highlanders		
Heading	7 Meerut Div 19 Dehradun Bde 4 Bn Seaforth Hdrs 1914 Aug-1915 Nov France To 51 Div-154 Bde		
Miscellaneous	Extracts From "Two Years With The 4th Bn Seaforth Highlanders"		
Miscellaneous	Copy of Private Diary Of 2/Lieut A.H.C Hope	01/11/1914	10/06/1915
Heading	Meerut Division Aug-Dec 1914 4d Seaford Hr Nov-Dec 1914		
Diagram etc	Diagram		
Heading	4 Bn Seaforth Hldrs 2 Nov 1914 To 6 Jany 1915		
Miscellaneous	Miscellaneous		
Heading	War Diary of 4th Battn Seaforth Highlanders From 2nd Nov 1914 To 6th Janry 1915		
War Diary	Bedford	02/11/1914	02/11/1914
War Diary	Le Havre	06/11/1914	06/11/1914
War Diary	Le Havre Bleville	07/11/1914	07/11/1914
War Diary	Le Havre	08/11/1914	09/11/1914
War Diary	Ecques	09/11/1914	22/11/1914
War Diary	Arques	23/11/1914	19/12/1914
War Diary	Vieille Chapelle	19/12/1914	26/12/1914
War Diary	Ferfay	27/12/1914	03/03/1915
Heading	Meerut Division 4th Seaforth Highlanders From 1st To 31st March 1915		
Heading	War Diary of 4th Seaforth Highlanders From 1st March 1915 To 31st March 1915		
War Diary		04/03/1915	31/03/1915
Heading	Meerut Division 4th Seaforth Highlander From 1st To 30th April 1915		
Heading	War Diary of 4th Seaforth Highlanders From 1st April 1915 To 30th April 1915		
Miscellaneous	Dehra Dun Brigade	14/04/1915	14/04/1915
War Diary	Summary of Evants etc	01/04/1915	30/04/1915
Heading	Meerut Division 1/4th Seaforth Highlanders April 30th To June 1st 1915		
Heading	War Diary 1/4th Seaforth Hdrs May 1915		
War Diary	Summary Of Events	30/04/1915	01/06/1915
Miscellaneous			
Heading	Meerut Division 1/4th Seaforth Highlanders From 1st June To July 3rd 1915		
Heading	War Diary of 1/4th Seaforth Highlanders From 1st June 1915 To 30th June 1915		
War Diary	Summary Of Events	02/06/1915	03/07/1915
Heading	Meerut Division 1/4th Seaforth Highlanders From July 1st To 1st August 1915		
Heading	War Diary of 4th Seaforth Highlanders From 1st July To 31st July 1915		
War Diary	Summary Of Events	04/07/1915	01/08/1915
Heading	Meerut Division 1/4 Seaforth Highlanders From 1st August To 1st Sept 1915		

Heading	War Diary Of 1/4th Seaforth Highlanders Form 1st August 1915 To 31st August 1915		
War Diary	Summary Of Events	01/08/1915	01/09/1915
Heading	Meerut Division 1/4th Seaforth Highlanders From 1st To 30th Sept 1915		
Heading	War Diary With Appendices Of 1/4th Seaforth Highlanders From 2nd September 1915 To 30th September 1915		
War Diary	Summary Of Events	01/09/1915	04/09/1915
Operation(al) Order(s)	Operation Order 54 by Lieut Colonel W.J. St. J. Harvey Commanding Dehra Dun Brigade.	16/09/1915	16/09/1915
Miscellaneous	Head Quarters Dehra Dun Brigade	16/09/1915	16/09/1915
Miscellaneous	Head Quarters Dehra Dun Brigade	17/09/1915	17/09/1915
Miscellaneous	Machine Gun Operation Orders	17/09/1915	17/09/1915
Miscellaneous	Movement Table	18/09/1915	18/09/1915
Miscellaneous	Head Quarters Dehra Dun Brigade	29/09/1915	29/09/1915
Miscellaneous	Head Quarters Dehra Dun Brigade	30/09/1915	30/09/1915
Miscellaneous	Instructions For Relief of Ind. 5.A. by Garhwal Brigade	20/09/1915	20/09/1915
Miscellaneous			
Miscellaneous	Instructions for Battalions of Dehradun Brigade on the day of assault	21/09/1915	21/09/1915
Miscellaneous	Operation Order 55 by Brigadier General W.J. St. J. Harvey Commanding Dehra Dun Bde.	23/09/1915	23/09/1915
Diagram etc	Diagram		
Operation(al) Order(s)	Operation Order No 56 by Brigadier General W.J. St. J. Harvey Commanding Dehra Dun Brigade.	22/09/1915	22/09/1915
Miscellaneous	Meerut Division	22/09/1915	22/09/1915
Miscellaneous	A Form, Messages And Signals		
Miscellaneous	Head Quarters Dehra Dun Brigade	22/09/1915	22/09/1915
Miscellaneous			
Miscellaneous	The O.C	23/09/1915	23/09/1915
Miscellaneous	Head Quarters Dehra Dun Brigade	23/09/1915	23/09/1915
Miscellaneous	A Form, Messages And Signals		
Miscellaneous			
Miscellaneous	A Form Messages And Signals		
Operation(al) Order(s)	Operation Order No 57 by Brigadier General W.J. St. J. Harvey Commanding Dehra Dun Brigade.	23/09/1915	23/09/1915
Miscellaneous	Movement Table		
Diagram etc	Diagram		
Miscellaneous	A Form, Messages And Signals		
Miscellaneous	Not To Be Carried Forward Beyond Our Front Parapet Under Any Circumstances		
Operation(al) Order(s)	Operation Order No. 58 by Brigadier General W.J. St. J. Harvey Commanding Dehra Dun Brigade.	24/09/1915	24/09/1915
Miscellaneous	Head Quarters Dehra Dun Brigade	24/09/1915	24/09/1915
Miscellaneous	A Form, Messages And Signals		
Miscellaneous			
Operation(al) Order(s)	Operation Order 59 by Brig Genl W.J. St. J. Harvey Comdg Dehra Dun Bde.	25/09/1915	25/09/1915
Miscellaneous	Programme for Rifle, Rifle Grenade and Machine Gun Fire	30/09/1915	30/09/1915
Heading	Meerut Division 1/4th Seaforth Highlander For October 1915		
Heading	Meerut 46th Division 1/4th Seaforth Highrs Oct 1915 Vol I		
Miscellaneous	1/4th Seaforth Highrs	03/11/1915	03/11/1915

War Diary	Summary Of Events	02/10/1915	31/10/1915
Heading	15th Division 46th Infy Bde 1-4th Bn Seaforth Hgdrs 1915 Nov-Dec 1915		
Miscellaneous	15th Division		
War Diary	Summary Of Events	01/11/1915	30/11/1915
Heading	1/4th Seaforth Highrs Dec Vol III		
War Diary		01/12/1915	31/12/1915
Miscellaneous	Proposed Facilities To Enable soldiers of the ? Expeditionary Force to invest in the War Loan.		

WO95/3941/2

4 Battalion Seaforth
Highlanders

7 MEERUT DIV

19 DEHRA DUN BDE

4th BN SEAFORTH HDRS

1914 AUG — 1915 NOV

FRANCE
TO 51 DIV — 154 BDE

EXTRACTS FROM "Two Years with the 4th Bn. Seaforth Highlanders"

by

E.C. Bessent (25 Marine Square, Kemp Town, BRIGHTON).

1914.

Sept, 4th. Enlisted in the 4th Seaforths (at London Scottish Headquarters).

8th. Moved with draft to Bedford. Commanding Officer Lt.-Col. D.M. Macfarlane.

Nov. 1st. Warned to be prepared for overseas.

3rd. Bn. inspected by Brigadier.

5th. Leave Bedford for Southampton and embark on the "City of Dunkirk"

6th. Arrive and berth in harbour at Le Havre.

7th. Disembark and march to camp at Bleville.

8th. Entrain at 10 a.m. from Le Havre.

9th. Arrive at St. Omer at 10.15 where Bn. ~~disentrained~~ detrained and march about 5 miles to Ecques where Bn. is billeted in barns etc.,

10thto 21st. Bn. employed Trench digging, battalion manoeuvres, rifle practice etc.

22nd. Bn. marched to Arques (about 8 miles from Ecques)

Dec. 16th. Bn. left Arcques at 9 a.m. and march to Lampres (about 1 mile from Aure) at 1 p.m.

17th. Left Lampres at 9 a.m. and march through Lillers and Chocques to Labouvriere (a distance of 15 miles) arriving at 3 p.m.

18th. Bn. marched at 9 a.m. from Labouvriere to Vieille Chapelle (about 8 miles).

20th. Inspected by Gen. Willcocks, commanding the Indian Corps.
Bn. received orders to move (at 1 p.m.) within half an hour and march about 2 miles to La Couture.
Bn. attached to Dehra Dun Brigade, Meerut Divn.

21st. Bn. took up position in reserve trenches, afterwards marching back to Vieille Chapelle.

22nd. Bn. went into reserve trenches at 4 p.m. behind 1st Seaforths and L.N.Lancs. Up to knees in mud and water. Very cold..

23rd. Bn. leaves trenches at 9 a.m. and Right Half goes in again in the afternoon. The left half (E.F.G. and H. companies) remain in billets at Vieille Chapelle.

24th. Right half battalion vacates trenches. Meerut

1914.

Dec. 24th cont'd. Division going out, to rest tomorrow.

25th. Bn. marched to Robec where it billeted.

26th. At 10 a.m. Bn. marched out of Robec, to Ferfay, a distance of about 12 miles where billets were occupied.

1915.

Early days of January spent in route marching, practice bomb throwing from the trenches. The G.O.C. inspected the Dehra Dun Brigade on the 7th January in a blinding snow and wind storm; on

Jan. 14th Battalion ordered to move, and left Ferfay at 4 p.m passing through Chocques and arriving at Vendin at 10 p.m. after a march of about 15 miles.

15th. Left Vendin at 11 a.m., passing through Bethune and La Couture and reaching Richebourg St. Vaast at 3.30 p.m.

16th. Bn. inspected by General Keary.

17th. Bn. moved to Richebourg Rue de Bois at 5 p.m. to relieve the Highland Light Infantry. On the way came under machine-gun fire, wounding several of the men.

18th. Sherwood Foresters are holding the line on our left and a Lancashire Regiment the right.

19th.
20th. Battalion was relieved by companies during these two days, by the 1st Manchester Regt.

22nd. Bn. left Lacouture at 11 a.m. reaching Vendin at 4 p.m.

23rd. Bn. left Vendin at 10.30 a.m. and arrived at Ferfay where it went into billets.

26th. Battalion ordered to "stand to" all night.

31st. Battalion left Ferfay at 9 a.m. and marched to Hinges (about 10 miles) where it stopped for the night.

Feb. 1st. Left Hinges at 9 a.m. and reached Richebourg St. Vaast at 12.30 p.m. F1 Company (Sections 1 & 2) go into a redoubt during the night.

2nd. Trench digging. Enemy snipers very alert. Several men wounded.

3rd. Trench digging and sandbag filling. D and E company's in the firing line.

4th. Bn. left Richebourg St. Vaast at 2.30 p.m. for Vieille Chapelle. Shelled during the march several men being killed or wounded.

5th. After being inspected by Gen. Jacobs (B.G.C.Dehra Dun Brigade) the Battn. marched to Colonne.

writer in hospital with measles till April

1915.

April 28th. Battalion moved to Vieille Chapelle (about 2 miles) in the evening.

May 8th. Battalion left Vieille Chapelle at 7 p.m. and went into the trenches at the Rue de Bois, Richebourg.

9th. Bombardment opened punctually at 5 a.m. When this stopped No. 1 coy was ordered to advance but were met with a heavy machine gun and rifle fire from the enemy only 80 yards off. No. 2 Coy were then ordered to advance but met the same heavy fire. During the advance Lieut. Tennant was killed and a number of other ranks killed and wounded, including Sergt. Menzies (both legs broken). Losses in the Battalion were estimated at 3 officers (Lieut,s Railton, Bastion and Tennant) and 216 men. About 11 p.m. the Bn. was relieved by the 58th Rifles.

11th. Bn. moved to Vieille Chapelle.

15th. Bn. inspected by the Brigadier who congratulates it on the prominent part it took in the recent attack.

16th. Battn. ordered to "stand to". Nothing however happened.

17th. Battn. standing to all day.

18th. Battalion moved at 8 p.m. to just beyond Croix Barbee, occupying some ploughed fields.

21st. Battn. returned to Vieille Chapelle.

23rd. Battn. left Vieille Chapelle at 6.30 p.m., going into the line at Richebourg Rue de Bois. Were shelled on the way several men being knocked out.

24th. In the line.

25th. Gas alarm given, and masks worn but the gas does not penetrate into the line.

June 2nd. Battn. moved into reserve trenches just behind Rue de Bois.

5th. 12 casualties were suffered in the Battn. while moving into dugouts near La Couture.

7th. Battn. moved into Vieille Chapelle.

12th. Battn. inspected by Gen Willcocksm G.O.C. Indian Corps.

17th. Battalion went into the line just to the right of the Rue de Bois, Richebourg.

22nd. Sir John Fowler (Adjutant) killed by a shell coming through top of dugout.

23rd. Battn. relieved in the front line by 1st Seaforths and go into reserve trenches.

29th. Battn. returns to trenches at the right of the Rue de Bois, Richebourg at 10 p.m.

1915.

June 30th. Bn. in the line. Shelling by the enemy.

July 1st. Stevenson shot through the head whilst on Sentry duty. Killed instantly.

3rd. Battn. relieved from the firing line by the 2/2 Gurkhas, and go into billets at Touret,

7th. Battn. left Touret at 10 p.m. and went into trenches near Richebourg Rue de Bois, companies No. 2 and 3 in the firing line, 4 in support, 1 in reserve.

9th. Two men of A coy wounded by a bomb.

10th. Battn. relieved at 10 p.m. by 2/Yorks. March through Richebourg, Vieille Chapelle to La Gorgue, arriving at about 2 a.m.

14th. Several new officers joined to-day. Battn. left La Gorgue at 8.30 p.m. and marching up the La Bassee road went into trenches at Neuve Chapelle. Raining heavily, communication trenches filled with water up to the men's knees. Companies 1 and 4 in firing line, 2 and 3 in support; in reserve are the 4/King's Liverpools; 1st Seaforths on right of Battn. and 1st Manchester on the left.

17th. Trenches shelled fairly heavily and several men wounded.

19th, Capt. Forsyth evacuated with nervous breakdown. A patrol of 4 men under Lieut. Harris went out towards the German line and returned without any mishap.

21st. Battn. relieved at 11 p.m. by the 47th Sikhs, and went into billets at Pont Duhem on the La Bassee road.

26th. Battn. left Pont Duhem at 9.30 p.m., No. 4 Coy going into Curzon Redoubt just behind Neuve Chapelle, 1, 2, and 3 remaining on the La Bassee road.

30th. Battn. went into billets at La Gorgue.

Aug. 8th. Battn. went into the firing line to left of Neuve Chapelle taking a double company of 10th Warwicks with them.

9th. Several men of the Bn. and Warwicks wounded by a bomb in a listening post.

10th. Patrol of four men went out as it was reported that a gap existed in the German wire. Returned in safety reporting that the enemy wire had not been cut.

12th. Battn. to billets at Pont Duhem.

14th. No. 2 and 3 Coys into firing line between Neuve Chapelle and Laventie, relieving the 6th Jats. No. 4 in reserve at a farm on the Bacquerot road.

1915.

Aug. 16th. No. 4 company moved into reserve trenches "Moated Grange".

17th. Digging party employed at headquarters were shelled suffering one killed and several wounded.

18th. No. 4 Coy to support trench near the "Birdcage" between Neuve Chapelle and Laventie.

20th. Battn. left trenches and returned to Pont Duhem.

24th. Battn. left Pont Duhem ("Rugby Road") at 8,p.m. and went into billets at La Gorgue.

29th. Battn. left La Gorgue at 7 p.m. and went into billets at Pont du Hem. A bomber of No. 1 Coy accidentally dropped a case of bombs in a barn which was crowded with men, one bomb exploded killing one man and wounding 17.

31st. Battn. digging communication trench just to left of Neuve Chapelle.

Sept. 1st. Battalion employed on carrying timber for dug-outs in the support line.

3rd. Battn. employed carrying ammunition to the line.

4th. Draft of 80 men arrive. Battn. relieved the 4/Black Watch in the line at night.

8th. Battn. relieved by Gurkhas and go into reserve trench between "Lafone" and "Moated Grange" communication trenches.

12th. Battn. left reserve trenches and went into billets at La Gorgue.

18th. Battn. left la Gorgue and went into the line at "The Duck's Bill".

20th. Pte McIver killed by a rifle bullet whilst coming out of a listening post.

25th. Attack by the Bareilly Brigade, the Dehra Dun Brigade being in support and the Garhwal Brigade on the right. One hundred of the Bn. were assisting the engineers in charge of gas cylinders and also with the smoke screen. Of these 11 were wounded and 20 gassed by our own gas. Raining heavily.

28th. Battn. left the line and went into billets between Vieille Chapelle and Lacouture.

Oct. 2nd. Battn. moved at 9 p.m. and went into trenches at Gorre, near Givemchy (after stopping at Beuvry).

14th. Battn. left the line and went into dug-outs about 2 miles behind Gorre.

21st. Battn. went into the trenches at Richebourg Rue de Bois.

24th. Battn lost 3 men killed and six wounded.

1915.

Oct. 24th (cont'd) Pte. Robertson recommended for the D.C.M. for going out in front (as a stretcher bearer) and bringing in Sergt. Rogers who was wounded.
At a late hour the Battn. was relieved from the firing line and went into billets at Paradis.

28th. At 9.30 a.m. Btn. moved off to be inspected with the Dehra Dun Brigade by the King, but as H.M. met with an accident Gen. Jacobs inspected the Brigade.
It was announced that Col. Macfarlane who commanded the Bn. at the Battle of Neuve Chapelle has been awarded the C.M.G., and Major Cuthbert the D.S.O. Pte. A. McLeod has been awarded the D.C.M. for voluntarily leaving his trench on 11th March and bandaging a seriously wounded Gurkha whilst under heavy m.g. and rifle fire.

Nov. 2nd. Battn. left Paradis at 10 a.m. and went into billets at King's Road, near Lacouture. Raining heavily all day.

3rd. A bomb burst in No. 1 Coy's billet killing Pte McKay, H. and wounding 3 others.

4th. Bn. parades before Gen. Jacobs who wishes the men "good-bye" on behalf of the Indian Army which is Leaving France.

5th. Battn. went into the trenches at Rue de Bois, Richebourg, No. 3 coy into the firing line at "The Glory Hole" and remainder in support and reserve trenches.

6th. Lt. Harrop shot through arm while going up communication trench.

7th. Pte. McCall killed instantly by bullet through the head.

10th. Pte. McIlroy killed, being taken by a sniper of the Sherwood Foresters for one of the enemy.

12th. Battn. moved about 8 miles to Calonne St. Lys, and went into billets.

16th. Battn. moved by lorries to Douvrin, and is attached to 46th Brigade, 15th Division, IV Corps, First Army.

18th. Draft of 150 arrived.

24th. Battn. moved to Loos and went into trenches near the Hohenzollern Redoubt, Hulluch.

26th. Battn. left the trenches and went into billets at Sailly Labourse.

28th, Battn. went into trenches at Loos.

30th. Battn. came out of the trenches, went into vaults at Vermelles.

Dec. 2nd. Battn in the line again.

4th. Battalion out of trenches and went into vaults at Vermelles.

1915.

Dec. 7th. Battn. moved to billets at Vaudricourt.

13th. Battn. left Vaudricourt at 8.30 a.m. and marched abt. 8 miles to Burbure where there were billets. 20th London took over billets at Vaudricourt.

The writer went on leave on Dec. 24th to England.

1916.

Jan. 6th. Battn. entrained at Lillers and arrived at Amiens at 9.30 p.m. Marhced about 9 miles to Cardonette where they were billeted.

7th. Battn. now in the 154th Brigade, 51st (Highland) Division.

11th to 23rd. Most of the time spent digging trenches.

25th. Inspected by G.O.C. of the Division.

29th. A party of 60 under Lieut. Robson left for Flessells (about 10 miles) to take part in a scheme.

From Jan. 30th to April 10th writer was in the Military Police.

Apr. 12th. Capt. McClintock (4th Gordons) in temporary command of Battn. Battn. in reserve. 4th Gordons in the front line.

15th. Draft of 180 men join the Battn. At 7 p.m. No. 2 Coy moved into the firing line at Roclincourt, between Arras (right) and Vimy Ridge (left).

17th. Artillery busy on both sides all day. No. 3 Coy went into firing line and No. 2 into support.

21st. Battn. relieved by 4/Gordons and go into billets at Etrun, being in reserve.

27th. Battn. moved into the trenches, 3 and 4 Coys going into firing line.

28th. Enemy fired a mine just on the left of Battn. 13 men wounded.

29th. L/Cpl. MacKenzie killed and several men wounded during "stand to" at early morning,

May 1st. 3 men of No, 1 Coy wounded by a bomb.

2nd. Walter ~~Lewis~~ Still (Lewis Gunner) slightly wounded by a bomb.

3rd. Battn. relieved by 4th Gordons and went into billets at Etrun.

9th. Battn. relieved 4th Gordons , No. 4 Coy going into the support line.

12th. No. 4 Coy into firing line.

14th. Trench bombed most of the day.

1916.

May 15th. 4/Gordons relieved Battn in the firing line, which returned to billets at Etrun in reserve.

21st. Battn. returned to trenches, No. 4 Coy in the support line.

23rd. Colonel Steuart, commanding officer killed by a bomb. He only joined Battn on the 15th.

24th. No. 4 Coy. moved up to firing line relieving No. 1 Coy.

25th to 28th. Heavy shelling and bombing by the enemy, and on the 28th reported gas shelling in the line.

29th. Two new Lewis guns arrive for battn. making a total of eight.

June 9th. Battn. relieved by 4/Gordons who march back to Etrun.

15th. Battn. relieved 4/Gordons in the trenches.

17th. Several of the men of battn. were killed by a bomb dropping in their midst whilst repairing the parapet.

21st. Battn. Relieved by 4/Gordons, and retire to reserve trenches at Ecurie.

28th. Battn. relieved 4/Gordons in the firing line Nos. 3 & 4 Companies in front, 1 & 2 in support.

The writer of the diary left the battalion to take up a commission on July 8th 1916.

COPY OF PRIVATE DIARY OF 2/LIEUT. A.H.C. HOPE,

4th (Ross Highland) Bn. Seaforth Highlanders (TF).

from 1st November 1914 to 10th June 1915.

1914.

Nov. 1st.	Telegram arrived from W.O. at 6.43 p.m. ordering Battn. abroad in company with 1st Herts and 5th Essex.
2nd to 4th.	Battn. equipping and preparing for overseas.
5th.	Battn. left Bedford 2.15 p.m arr. Southampton about 7 p.m. Embarked on Transport "City of Dunkirk" at 8.30 p.m., after the issue of first field dressings.
7th.	Landed at Le Havre, after a night spent in harbour, at 8.30 a.m. and marched to camp No. 2 arriving about 11.0 a.m.
8th.	Entrained at 1.20 p.m. and arrived at Rouen at 5 p.m. and after a wait proceeded (by train) to St. Omer which was reached at 11.30 a.m. on the 9th.
9th.	Marched from St. Omer to Ecques, 9.5 km. south-east of St. Omer which was reached about 3 p.m. and the battn. billeted.
10th to 21st.	Battn. on exercise, outpost duty, practice shooting, company drill, and entrenchment work.
22nd.	Battn. left Ecques and marched to Arques, about a mile from St. Omer where they billeted.
23rd & 24th.	Battn. spent time entrenching.
25th to 30th.	Battn. engaged on entrenching, field firing and practice attacks.
Dec. 1st to 15th.	do. do. do. do.
16th.	Battn moved to Lombres, via Aire, a distance of about 11¼ miles.
17th.	Battn. moved to Labeuvriere, about 12-14 miles arriving abt. 2.30 p.m.
18th.	March continued at 9 a.m. to Vieille Chapelle arriving at about 1 p.m. Very wet day.
20th.	Battn. inspected by Gen. Willcocks, commanding Indian Corps at 12.30. At 2.15 the battn. moved off to support, about 3 miles away.
21st. to 23rd.	Battn. in reserve trenches (part of the Rue du Bois), returning to billets abt midday on the 23rd.

1914.

Dec. 25th. Battn. moved off at 8.10 am to Rebecq.

26th. Moved off at 10 a.m. for Ferfay.

1915.

Jan. 4th. Battn. inspected in the afternoon by Gen. Wilcocks of 19th Bde.

14th. Battn. moved to Vendin about 3 p.m. arriving there abt. 9 p.m.

15th. Paraded at 11 a.m. and marched to Richebourg St. Vaast, arriving about 3 p.m. and going into billets.

17th. Battn. paraded at 4.30 p.,. in Richebourg and proceeded to the trenches east of the Rue du Bois.

20th. Battn. relieved by 3 coys Manchesters and one coy Suffolks about 2.30 a.m. and marched to Lacouture arriving about 4.30 when they billeted.

22nd. Left Lacouture at 11.30 a.m. for Vendin which was reached at 4 p.m.

23rd. Moved to Ferfay.

31st. Moved to Hinges at 9 a.m. Snowing.

Feb. 1st. March continued to Richebourg St. Vaast, arriving at noon.

4th. Moved to Vieille Chapelle.

8th. Inspected by Gen. Jacobs at 10.40 a.m. Marched through Vieille Chapelle to Calonne.

Writer was on leave in England from 15th Feb to 23rd Feb.

March 2nd. Battn. relieved by 41st Dogras at 6.30 p.m. and marched to old billets at Vieille Chapelle and Lacouture.
Draft of 2 officers and 55 men arrived from Bedford.

10th. Battn. moved at 3 a.m. to redoubts just east of Richebourg St. Vaast where they stayed till about 10 a.m.
Later the coys moved on, and Major Robertson, Col.-Sergt. Bell and about 20 other ranks of No. 1 Coy were wounded, the officer subsequently died of his wounds.
About 4 p.m. battn. moved up and eventually reached Neuve Chapelle about 10 p.m.

11th. Col. MacFarlane (C.O.) wounded about 10 a.m.
3.0 p.m. ordered to advance.
Capt. Findlay and several o.r. killed. The total casualties on 10th and 11th were :-
Killed, Capt. R.de C Findlay; Died of Wounds, Major W.J. Robertson, Capt. Budge, Lieut. J.Macmillan. Wounded, Lt.Col. D. Mason Macfarlane, Major Cuthbert, Capt. R. Truslove, Lieut. A.B. Brook. O.R's about 160.

12th. Battn. relieved by H.L.I. and returned to Vieille

1915.

March 12th. Chapelle arriving about 5 a.m. Moved again at 6.45 a.m. to Lestrem, and about 6 p.m. marched to Richebourg, arriving there about 11.30 p.m.

15th. Inspected by Gen. Anderson, commanding Meerut Divn.

16th. Inspected by Gen. Sir James Willcocks.

21st. to 23rd. Draft of 150 men arrived on 22nd. No officers with them.

24th. Dehra Dun Brigade moved up to trenches just north of Neuve Chapelle. Battn moved at 7 a.m.

27th. Capt. Ferguson, 2/Lieuts. Macleod, Pender, Hulls and Cartwright arrived from England. Battn. relieved 1st Seaforths

30th. Battalion relieved by Connaught Rangers and a coy of the 3rd London Regt., and went into billets between Vieille Chapelle and Croix Barbe.

31st. Moved at 4 p.m. to Croix Marmuse, via Vieille Chapelle, Pont Levis.

April 11th. Battn. relieved 5/Sussex and a coy 2/Sussex in Neuve Chapelle about 12 midnight. No's 1 and 2 in reserve, 3 and 4 in firing line.

27th. Battn. relieved by 39th Garhwalis with exception of machine guns, and went back to billets near Vieille Chapelle, R29.

28th. 2083 Pte. P.M. Dent shot through the head about 7.5 p.m. and succumbed about 10 p.m. whilst being moved to the dressing station, so was moved to the church redoubt in the village for the night.

30th. Battn. issued with Balmoral bonnets. 4 D.C.M's including Minchin. A very quiet day.

May 1st. The enemy commenced shelling lines at Neuve Chapelle, Port Arthur and the Rue du Bois a little after 4 a.m. , causing few casualties to 1st Battn. G. Coys billet on fire about 8.30 p.m.and despite assistance the building was destroyed but the remainder were saved.

3rd. Major Fraser appointed D.A.Q.M.G. at Calais; Capt. D.A. Mackenzie appointed A.M.L.O. C. Calais.

5th. Inspection at 11.30 a.m.

7th. 1/Cpl. Shaw wounded through the back (died later).

8th. Battn. in the line about 11 p.m.

9th. Bombardment began, cutting wire till 5.20 and then lifting to the trench line. At 5.30 our first line (A & C Coys) went over the parapet and were met with heavy rifle and m.g. fire. A few minutes later the second line (B & G Coys) went over and met the same resistance, making advance quite out of the question. One maxim hit through breech casing almost at once.

1915.

May 9th. Of the officers of the Battn. the following were wounded:- Railton & Macdonald (badly); Cameron(severe shoulder wounds) Knight and Pender; and Watt, slightly wounded. Killed, or believed killed:- Bastian and Charles Tennant. Railton, who was missed by the stretcher bearers was found a couple of days later, killed by shrapnel.
Battn. relieved about 4 p.m. and got down to S t. Vaast post leaving the trenches abt. 5.30 p.m. for Riez Bailleul near Estaires where they arrived about 8,p.m. About one third of the battalion was killed or wounded.

10th. Muster Parade at 11 a.m.
Draft of 27 o.r. under 2/Lt. Harris arrived from Rouen.

11th. Dehra Dun Brigade moved to Vieille Chapelle in the afternoon, arriving about 4.30 p.m.

15th. Muster parade at 10 a.m.

16th. Stood to arms all day.

18th. Dehra Dun Brigade moved in evening from Vieille Chapelle to Rue du Puits, between Rouge Croix and Croix Barbee at 8.15. p.m. Battn. went into a roughly made trench about 200 yds east of road, opposite Meerut Div.H.Q. midway along Rue du Puits..

19th. About 4 a.m. the coys were brought back to the road and put into billets.

21st. Dehra Dun Bde. moved back to Vieille Chapelle, 1/4th Seaforths marching off by coys at 5.0 p.m. with 15 minute intervals.

23rd. Battn. moved up to the trenches at 6.30 p.m. Proceeded up Queen Mary's road, Rue des Berceaux to Windy Corner and Edward road. Whilst on the way up enemy shelled with shrapnel, wounding L/Cpl. Allason and Pte. P. Fraser, (slight).

24th. Strengthening parapet at bridge, making latrines, cutting a deeper path from bridge to trench.

24th. Stood to at 2.30 a.m.
Pte C. Sutherland, F Coy struck in the head by a bullet about 4.30 a.m.
About 7.40 p.m. Lieut. Daman was shot in the head by a sniper and killed instantly. Two gas alarms in the night.
Between 9 and 10 p.m. enemy commenced shelling again a couple of shells bursting over our line almost right above the listening post. Pte. H. Veryard wounded (leg broken by a piece of the casing).

25th. Gas alarm about 8.15 p.m., but gas passed harmlessly aside.

26th. 1st Seaforths took over firing line from 4th Seaforths about 8.30 p.m. the latter retiring to dugouts between Windy Corner and Lansdowne Post.

June 2nd. 1/4th Seaforths relieved 6th Jats in trenches in front of Albert Road.

1915.

June 6th. Battn. came down about 10 p.m. and all went into trenches at Cour St. Vaast for the afternoon.

7th. Battn. relieved by 1/3rd London Regt. about 3 p.m. Billets between Port Levis, Vieille Chapelle and Zelobes.

9th. Battn. paraded by coys for route marches and bathing.

Diary ends June 10th.

Meerut Division Aug-Dec 1914

4th Seaforth Hrs.

Nov - Dec 1914

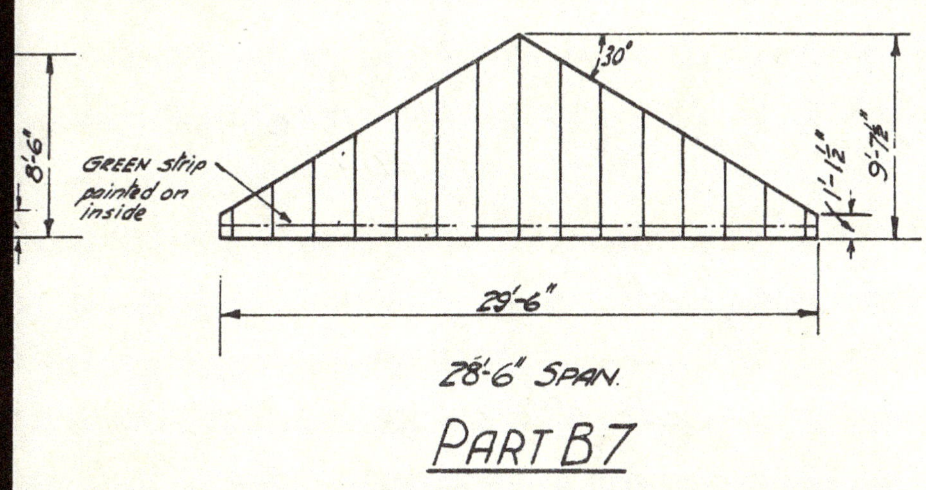

28'-6" SPAN.

PART B7

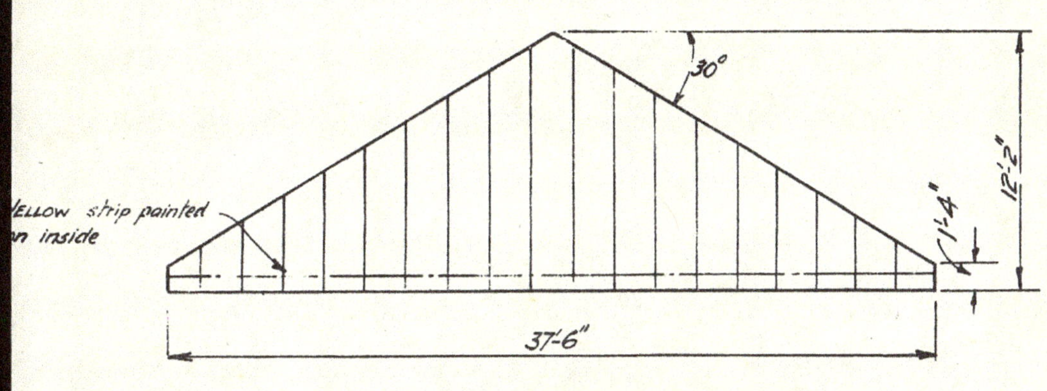

36'-6" SPAN

PART B8

SETS OF EXTERNAL GABLE SHEETING

WHEN FIXED

n fixed they conform to the dimensions shown.
be clearly marked by means of a 6" coloured
indicated
s × 24 gauge, & to be laid with single side laps.

AMENDED 19-10-38.

SHEETS. DRAWING No. H. 356/37

Dehra Dun
Meerut

4 Bn Seaforth Hldrs.

2 Nov 1914

to

6 Jany 1915.

Index

SUBJECT.

No.	Contents.	Date.
	The HON. ARTILLERY COMP'Y. — WAR DIARY, ~~AUG.~~ SEPT - DEC, 1914	

(56,425). Wt.24,741—161. 2000. 11/20. Gp.164. A.&E.W.

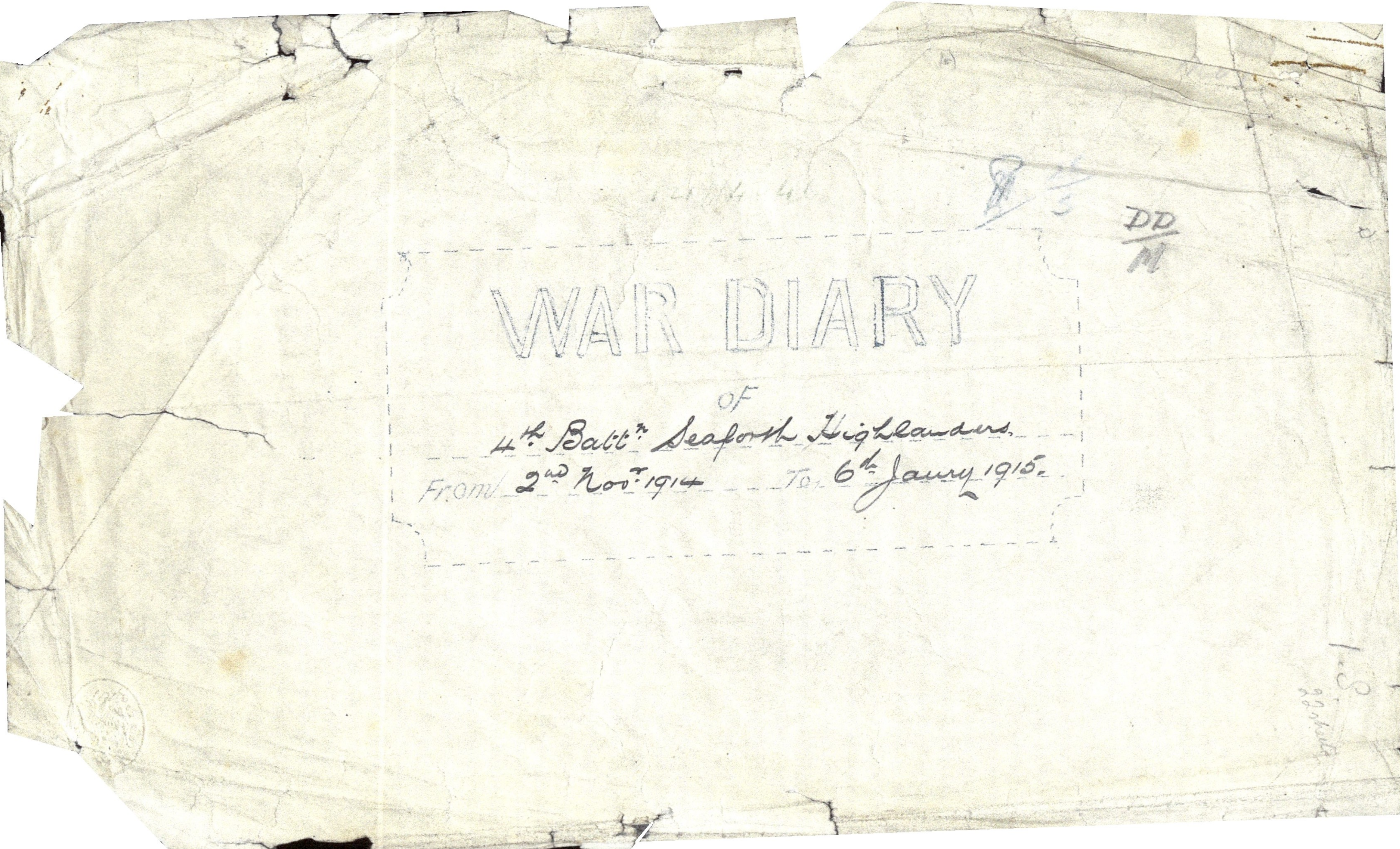

DD/M

WAR DIARY

OF

4th Battn Seaforth Highlanders.

From 2nd Novr 1914 To 6th Janury 1915.

1.S.

22 sheets

Hour, date, & place	Summary of events & information	Remarks & references to appendices.
Nov. 2 (BEDFORD)	Preparations for departure, filling up deficiencies in equipment	
Nov. 3 (BEDFORD)	" "	
Nov. 4 (BEDFORD)	" "	
Nov. 5. (BEDFORD)	The Bn. moved from Bedfd. in two halves starting from the Grammar School at 11.40 a.m. & 12.25 p.m. It arrived at Southampton Docks travelling by way of Oxford & Basingstoke, at between 7 & 8 p.m. and embarked on the City of Dunkirk an hour & a half afterwards. The men slept in the hold which was very roughly fitted up for their accommodation. The passage was very calm: during it, service jackets & boots were distributed & other refitting proceeded with. The City of D. which was one of a number of transports on this passage reached the harbour of Le Havre at Mid-day on	

1

Nov. 6.
LE HAVRE

Nov. 6. The Bn. paraded on deck at 2 o'clock p.m. ready to disembark, but, after waiting all afternoon for orders from the disembarking authorities & receiving none, again went to rest in the hold and other parts of the ship which was now in a dirty condition, no proper accommodation for sleeping having been provided. At 11 p.m. the ship proceeded to lay alongside the quay.

Nov. 7.
LE HAVRE
BLEVILLE

At 8.30 a.m. the Bn landed & were guided through Le Havre to Rest Camp ([illegible]) No 2 at Bléville, where it arrived at mid-day. In the afternoon a cursory inspection of kit was made by the Camp Commandant & a hasty indent for a number of deficient articles made up. ~~This camp was a [illegible] place with [illegible] kind.~~ The weather was also gloomy but not cold. In the evening orders were received to entrain next morning.

Nov. 8 A start from camp was made at 7.30 a.m.
LE HAVRE The Bn marched to the Gare des Marchandises & entrained at 1 o'clock, the loading of the transport waggons being a matter of some difficulty owing to the limited number of trucks & the necessity for careful fitting of the waggons & carts into the same: also the loading had to be done by means of inclined ramps.

A long & wearisome journey in a closely packed train followed: the route was via Rouen to Abbeville which was reached at 3 a.m. on Nov. 9

Nov. 9. At Abbeville meat, biscuits, tea & jam

2

Nov 9 (continued) were served out, these being the first regular rations since the previous morning. The train left Abbeville at 4.30 a.m. & proceeded to Etaples, thence to Boulogne & Calais which it skirted, reaching St Omer at 10.30 a.m.

ECQUES From St Omer the Bn. marched to billets allotted to it at the village of Ecques (some 6 m. S. of St O.) which it reached about 3 p.m. The billets were chiefly in barns, breweries & the like: the coy. HQrs & alarm post were on the muddy central square. The village was small (about 400 inhabitants in the central group of houses) but straggling & its resources were few. The worst of the billets were wretched: the best were indifferent: the sanitation was French.

2

Nov. 10. ECQUES	Battalion training took place in the morning on the ground to the S.E. of the village. The attack in "diamond formation" was the pièce de résistance of the training for the next 10 days. In the evening outposts were put out on the roads leading out of the village to the S.E. & E. Half a company forming two pickets, half a company in support in its billets. These outposts were put out every night.
Nov. 11. ECQUES	An early start was made for BLENDECQUES a village $1\frac{1}{2}$ m. S. of St. OMER. Here the Bn. practised entrenching, completing trenches already begun. Dimensions of trenches were as follows: fire trenches 12 to 15 ft. in length with traverse 6 ft. square between them. ~~These trenches were [illegible] the [illegible] in case of [illegible] by the Allies~~

Nov [illegible] ECQUES	The weather was cold and ~~rainy~~ windy + the Bn. reached its quarters at 5.30 p.m. in the rain.
Nov 12 ECQUES.	Route march to HEURINGHEM via INGHEM + HELFAUT (march discipline inspected by Gen. Chichester who professed himself satisfied). This was followed by an attack on Ecques in two lines of companies. In the afternoon re-arrangement of billets with a view to improving accommodation as far as possible. Cold & windy.
Nov. 13 ECQUES	Bn. exercise: attack on ROQUETOIRE which was curtailed by heavy rain: Drying of clothes difficult: mud in Ecques is deplorable.

Hour, date & place	Summary of events & information	Remarks & refs. to appendices
Nov 14 ECQUES	Trench digging to N. of BLENDECQUES: start at 7.30 a.m. Return at 4 p.m. Cold, windy with heavy showers at intervals	
Nov 15. ECQUES.	A day of rain & therefore of rest. Three cases of scarlet fever were taken into hospital at St OMER to day	
Nov 16. ECQUES	Heavy rain in the morning; in the intervals of wh. grouping on an extemporized range to the S.E. of the village was carried out. This was the first occasion of firing the new rifles issued at Bedford. Rain stopped operations in the afternoon. The muddy roads & fields made inroads on the men's boots which now began to give way	

Hour, date and place	Summary of events & information	Remarks & refs. to appendices
Nov 17. ECQUES	Grouping practices were continued but were much interrupted by rain. On this day the funeral of Ld. Roberts took place at St. OMER.	
Nov 18. ECQUES	A somewhat drier day in the morning Bn. practice in the attack: in the afternoon a route march which finished at 7 p.m., the last $1\frac{1}{2}$ hours giving an opportunity of practise in night marching.	
Nov 19. ECQUES	Practise in field firing by Companies	
Nov 20. ECQUES.	Practice in field firing by Companies & in the attack for those not so occupied.	

Hour, Date & Place	Summary of events & information.	Remarks & refs. to appendices
ECQUES Nov. 21.	Practice in the attack in the presence of Gen. Chichester, who ordered that in future the double company system should be adopted so far as work in the field was concerned. Hard frost. Considerable sickness owing to the dampness of previous days & wear & tear of boots.	
Nov. 22.	Owing to the unsatisfactory nature of the billets at ECQUES, the Bn. moved to quarters at ARQUES 3K. S. of St. OMER. This meant an improvement for many companies. The frosty weather necessitated re-shoeing of the transport & therefore much delay: but the move which began at 10 was completed by 7 p.m. ⌗	

Hour, Date & Place	Summary of events & information	Remarks & refs. to appendices
ARQUES Nov. 23	Entrenching in severely frosty weather to the S. of BLENDECQUES: an attack practice towards BLENDECQUES followed: return to billets at 3.30.	
Nov. 24.	Range practice on the 200^x range at St OMER. the 18 worst shots from each Coy. fired: the remainder practised fire direction & passing of messages.	
Nov. 25th.	attack practice from BELLE CROIX (S. of Arques) towards EBBLINGHEM. Heavy ploughs & much mud to move over: the attack was diversified by the fact that there was a canal to cross: one $\frac{1}{2}$ bn. moved over the bridge under cover of the fire of the other $\frac{1}{2}$.	

[illegible] date & place	Summary of events & information	Remarks & refs. to appendices
ARQUES Nov. 26.	Practice in marching through wooded country in the Forêt de CLAIRMARAIS, E. of St. Omer. Issue of boots on return to quarters: there were still many deficiencies in this respect.	
Nov. 27.	Rest day.	
Nov. 28.	Entrenching on the Canal Bank to SE of ARQUES. About 7.30 p.m. a dispatch was received to the effect that the Bn. was to move next day to LOCON to join the Dehra Dun Division of the Indian corps. This order was immediately followed by another to the effect that the renewed outbreak of scarlet fever reported this morning in the Bn. ~~made~~ cancelled the move for the present.	[illegible] / [illegible] Bde

Hour, Date & Place	Summary of events & information	Remarks & refs. to appendices
ARQUES Nov. 29	Field-firing & training by companies till 1 p.m.	
Nov 30.	Rain interfered with the operations of the Bn. which returned to its quarters soon after its start.	
Dec 1.	Bn. training in the attack; Bn. Drill; & company training from [illegible] a.m. to [illegible] p.m.	
Dec 2.	Practice in entrenching completing trenches begun on Nov. 28 close to Campagne (Pont de Campagne). Departure 8.15. Return 4 p.m.	

[Ho]ur, Date & place	Summary of events & information	Remarks & refs. to appendix
[A]RQUES Dec 3.	Rain interfered with work which was abandoned early in the morning.	
Dec 4.	Practice in field firing with special reference to the supply of ammunition, which was taken up to the firing-line by the reserve section of each company. Three cases of scarlet fever & one of mumps were [reported].	
Dec 5.	Torrential rain in the morning prevented ~~all~~ training during the day.	
Dec 6.	Sunday Church parade conducted by the Colonel. By the close of the day 3 companies were isolated on account of scarlet fever or mumps	
Dec 7.	A day of rain.	

12

Hour, date & place	Summary of events & information	Remarks & references to appendices
Dec. 8.	Digging at Fort Rouge; west of Renescure: trenches of usual type, except that traverse was 6' x 4'6" instead of 6' x 6'.	
Dec 9.	Rain prevented the Bn. leaving Arques.	
Dec. 10.	Attack by 5 coys. upon trenches dug on Dec 8. These trenches were held by A C. & G, the "isolated" companies.	
Dec. 11.	The trenches begun on Dec 8. were completed and others begun close to them.	
Dec. 12.	Rearguard action between B D E F H Coys. & A. C. G coys (alleged infections) on the road to Aire.	
Dec. 13.	Sunday.	

Hour, date & place	Summary of events & information	Remarks & reference to appendices
ARQUES Dec 14.	Digging trenches near Pont de Campagne	
Dec 15.	Rain prevented out door training. Preparations for departure.	
Dec 16.	Start at 9.5. Lambres (1½ m. S. of Aire) was reached at 12.45 & the Bn billeted there.	
Dec 17.	Start at 9. March by way of Lillers & Chocques to Labeuvrière (reached at 2 p.m.); here the Bn. billeted.	
Dec 18.	Start at 9. March by way of Béthune & Locon to Vieille Chapelle, which for the next week was the headquarters of the Bn.	
Dec 19.	Spent in billets. Orders to A & B Coys	

Hour, date & place	Summary of events & information	Remarks & references to appendices
Vieille Chapelle Dec 19 (continued)	to move on following day to the trenches for training in trench fighting by platoons.	
Dec 20.	Orders to A & B Coys cancelled; half the Bn (A & B + C & G) moved at 2 pm. to reserve trenches close to La Couture; the other ½ Bn. occupied billets at La Couture	
Dec 21.	& on the next day relieved the other two double coys. The trenches were situated between the road & the brook to the W & N.W of the R in RICHEBOURG. Heavy rifle & gun fire went during the whole night along the front. The Bn had on its left the 104th Gehrwal rifles. The Bn received orders to return to Vieille Chapelle about 7.30 p.m. on Dec 21.	
Dec 22.	On this day another sudden order was received to occupy the trenches near La Couture	

Hour, date & place	Summary of events & information.	Remarks & references to appendices.
	The Bn. marched at 3 o'clock & occupied the trenches during the night.	
Dec 23.	The Bn. marched off to Vieille Chapelle at 9.30 a.m. with the prospect of resting during the day but at 2 p.m. orders were received that half the Bn. should march off by way of Richebourg l'Avoué to trenches some 400x behind the firing line which it was to occupy & improve. The trenches which were behind the actual firing line of the 6th Gurkhas were occupied in reliefs of 3 hours by two single coys, the other two coys. billeting in shell-riddled barns close by. Stray shots came over the trenches & probably some sniping went on. Habitués however from other regiments denied this.	

Hour, date & place	Summary of events & information	Remarks & refs. to appendices
Dec 24.	The ½ Bn. did not occupy the trenches during the morning: the near neighbourhood of C & C coys'. billets was visited by shrapnel about 1.30. p.m. The ½ Bn. left for Vieille Chapelle at 3 p.m. and was met on its arrival by the news that its Division was to be rested. Orders were received during the course of the night to march to Robecq on the 25.	
Dec 25.	A hard frost. The Bn. reached Robecq (some 10 m. W. of Vieille Chapelle) at mid-day & went into billets for the night.	
Dec 26.	A start was made for Ferfay (4 m. S.W. of Lillers) (at 10 AM) which was reached about 2 p.m. The Billets were inferior, the Clearing Hospital ~~[illegible]~~ & Brigade H.Q. being also quartered in the village.	

Hour, date & place	Summary of events & information	Remarks & ref. to appendices
FER[illegible]AY		
Dec 27.	Sunday. Divine services under the newly-joined chaplain, the Rev. MacLeod.	
Dec 28, 29, 30, 31.	Rifle inspections, cleaning up, refitting &c. On the 29th the 1st Bn. passed thro' Ferfay on its way to billets at the neighbouring village of Amminval. New Year's Eve was celebrated by concerts under coy. arrangement, lasting till 12 midnt.	
1915 Jan 1.	In the afternoon Bn. sports in conjunction with the 1st Bn. were held.	
Jan 2 & 3.	No Bn. parades.	
Jan 4.	The Dehra Dun Brigade was inspected by Gen. Willcocks.	
Jan 5.	A wet day: Lecture to officers on entrenching by Lieut. Bird R.E. The Colonel left for a week's leave in England.	
Jan 6.	The Officers were introduced to General Jacobs, the	

Meerut Division

4th Seaforth Highlanders

From 7th Jan 1915. To 3rd March 1915

No. 261

12/14719

WAR DIARY

OF

~~1st~~ 4th Seaforth Highlanders.

From 7th January 1915 To 3rd March 1915

BR
10/3.

2.S.
11 sheets

Hour, Date, Place	Summary of events and information	Remarks and references to appendices
FERFAY	newly-appointed Brigadier. Route marching by Double Coys.	
Jan 7.	Indian army corps inspected by Gen. French	
Jan 8.	Siting of trenches on the Ammeval road. Bn. route march	
Jan 9.	Siting of trenches with help of practical advice from Capt. Murray (1st Seaforths). Practice in bomb throwing. Route march to Hurighem & back.	
Jan 10.	Bn. church parade at 10.45.	
Jan 11, 12, 13	Practise at entrenching, bomb throwing &c under advice of Seaforth (1st Bn) officers & non-coms. On the afternoon of the 13th we were informed that we were temporarily attached to the Sirhind Bgde. of the Lahore Divn.	
Jan 14.	Entrenching in the morning. In the afternoon the	

Hour, date & place	Summary of events & information	Remarks & refs to appendices
FERFAY Jan 14.	Bn received orders to join the Sirhind Bgde & left Ferfay at 4.30 for Vendin-les-Béthune where it billeted about 9 p.m.	
Jan 15.	Start at 11 a.m. to march via Béthune to Richebourg St Vaast which was reached at 3.30 p.m. Captain G. Fraser with two Maxims joined the H.L.I. at Richebourg L'Avoué. The Officers were introduced to General Keary, ~~the Bn~~ G.O.C. Division.	
Jan 16.	Bn rested in forenoon. Double Coy commanders visited the position at Richebourg l'Avoué. Gen Keary inspected the Bn in the afternoon.	
Jan 17	Church service in the morning. In the afternoon three double companies ~~start~~ moved to Richebourg-l'Avoué. C & G were in reserve at billets in cross-roads above S in DES of Rue des Berceaux (B series Sheet 36 S.W.). The Bn relieved	

Hour, Date & Place	Summary of events & information.	Remarks & refs. to Appendices
Jan 17.	the [illegible] in trenches S.E. of the Rue Du Bois. These were in places in a muddy & waterlogged condition.	
Jan 18.	Firing was kept up throughout the day but no incident of importance took place. The village was shelled in the neighbourhood of Lieut. Macmillan's position. Arrangements for working & [illegible] the relief were carried out at Richebourg St. Vaast.	
Jan 19-20	In the night the Manchesters and Suffolks relieved us. The Bn was clear of the village by 5 a.m. on Wed. morning and arrived at La Couture in Detachments during the morning and rested during the remainder of the day.	
Jan 21.	Cleaning & repose.	
Jan 22.	Left La Couture at 11.30 a.m. & marched with the brigade to Vendin-lès-Béthune (the billets of the Bn. itself).	

Hour, date, place	Summary of events & information	Remarks & refs to Appendices
Jan. 23.	Marched from Vendin at 10 a.m. and reached Ferfay at 3 p.m. via Marles-les-Mines & Cauchy. ~~The Bn.~~	
Jan. 24.	Divine Service. Inspection of rifles & clothing: making up indents for deficiencies.	
Jan. 25.	" " " " . Washing. To-day orders were received to the effect that the Bn. was attached for the time being to the Sirhind Brigade, that there was sharp fighting in front of the 1st. Army Corps & that the Bn. was to hold itself in constant readiness to move.	
Jan. 26.	Cleaning up during day: at 9 p.m. orders were received to pack up & be ready to move at half an hour's notice. There was however no move.	
Jan. 27.	Two hours Coy. drill in forenoon: the half-hour notice was changed to two hours notice. Afternoon utilized for instruction of specialists (Bomb throwers &c) weather fine & frosty.	

Hour, date, place.	Summary of events & information	Remarks & refs. to appendices.
Jan 28.	Right half battalion marched into Lillers by platoons to bathe. Remainder did battalion drill. Frost continues	
Jan 29.	Left half battalion bathed at Lillers. Coy. drill for remaining half which was also inspected by the Colonel.	
Jan 30.	Coy. drill in morning. Orders to rejoin Dehra Dun Bgde. ~~[illegible]~~ received in afternoon.	
Jan 31.	Left Ferfay 9 a.m. Arrived Hinges 1.30 p.m where we billeted. Snow during march.	
Feb. 1.	Left ~~Ferfay~~ Hinges at 9 a.m. reached billets at Richebourg St Vaast at 1 p.m. Capt. G. W. Fraser relieved 6th Jats machine guns in Rue de Bois at 6 p.m. On this day we rejoined Dehra Dun Brigade (1st & 4th Seaforths 2nd & 9th Gurkhas.). Capt. Budge commanded a fatigue party of A & B Coys to carry hurdles &c for redoubt in Rue de Bois. Lieut. Fitzroy with half of F Coy formed a guard for redoubt W. of Rue de Berceaux.	

Hour, Date & place	Summary of events & information	Ref. to appendices
Feb 2.	D & E Coys. relieved the portion of the Gurkhas in the trenches S. of the Rue du Bois. A party consisting of contingents from each of the other Coys. under Capt. Cameron for work on reserve trenches in the Rue du Bois. Casualties :- one dangerously wounded & 2 or 3 slightly wounded	
Feb 3.	Digging party from A & B Coys. worked at redoubts E. & W. of Rue des Berceaux. Richebourg St Vaast was shelled in evening about 7 o'clock	
Feb 4.	Bn. left Richebourg at 2.15 & went to billets on road between Vieille Chapelle & La Couture.	
Feb 5.	Bn. under Company arrangements. Bn. is first in waiting.	
Feb 6.	Bn under Coy. arrangements. ~~[illegible]~~ A party of 150 men of A & B Coys (+ a few of C & D) proceeded to	

Hour, date & place	Summary of events & information.	Remarks & refs. to appendices
	the Rue de Bois to make breastworks & protection for the main street.	
Feb. 7	Digging parties provided for C & G. & F & D.	
Feb. 8.	General Jacob addressed the Bn. on the subject of discipline &c. At 11 the Bn. moved from Vieille Chapelle & reached its billeting area near Calonne at 1 p.m. Here it expects to remain for 10 or 12 days.	
Feb 9	Bn. under Coy. arrangements.	
Feb. 10.	Bn. under Coy arrangements; section drill, route marches.	
Feb 11.	Bn. route march to Merville.	
Feb 12. 13.	Bn. under Coy. arrangements. A case of diphtheria occurred in A Coy.	

Hour, date, place.	Summary of events & information.	Remarks & refs. to appendices
Feb 14.	Church Parade by Coys.	
Feb 15	Coys. under Coy arrangement.	
Feb 16.	Route march to Robecq.	
Feb 17.	Rain.	
Feb 18	Coys. under Coy arrangements.	
Feb 19.	Route march to Merville.	
Feb 20.	Companies under company arrangements.	
Feb 21.	Church Parade.	
Feb 22.	Left Calonne 9.5 : reached Vieille Chapelle 12:30.	
~~Tuesday~~ Feb 23	Took over (from 47th Sikhs) section of the Rue du Bois	

Hour, date & place	Summary of events & information.	Remarks & refs to appendices
Feb 23 (continued), 24, 25, 26.	line running from Albert road to King Edward Rd: the right half battalion went into firing line with left half in reserve. Five sentry groups were posted in A or observation line, with other groups in B line (the line of resistance. Two reliefs in the 24 hours. There was little rifle fire during this tour of duty but the Rue du Bois was shelled regularly twice or three times a day. Digging parties from the reserve half battalion were employed during the evenings in strengthening the breastworks of the B line: & the ~~half~~ half-battalion in the firing line spent the 2 hours before daylight & the 2 hours after dusk in various tasks of the same kind. The Leicester regiment and subsequently the Black Watch held the line to the right of the Battalion.	

Hour, date & place	Summary of events & information	Remarks & refs. to appendices
Feb 27.	D. & [illegible]. Companies took over a piece of the line to the N.E of the right section from the 2nd Gurkhas.	
Feb 28.	F & H. Coys. relieved C. & G.	
March 1.		
March 2.	The Bn. handed over its section to the 37th Dogras between 6 & 8. p.m. & marched back to Vieille Chapelle. The first draft from the Reserve Bn. arrived under command of Capt. MacKinnon with Lieut. Summers.	
March 3.	Resting. A party 250 men carried out digging during the night in the vicinity of Port Arthur.	
~~March 4.~~		

Meerut Division

4th Seaforth Highlanders

From 1st To 31st March 1915

Serial No. 261

121/5114

WAR DIARY

OF

~~14th~~ 4th Seaforth Highlanders.

From 1st March 1915 To 31st March 1915

Hour, date & place	Summary of events & information	Remarks & refs to appendices
March 4.	[illegible] officers visited & inspected defences at & close to Port Arthur. No 4 Coy. moved into reserve at Richebourg owing to a sudden emergency but were recalled the same day. Carrying party from No 1 Coy. proceeded to neighbourhood of Port Arthur for night work	
March 5.	Companies under Company arrangements: attack practise. Carrying party detailed from No 4 Coy. for night work.	
March 6.	Attack practice under Coy. commanders interfered with by rain.	
March 7.	Sunday. Church parade of Companies at billets during afternoon. Carrying party of 200 men (made up from Nos 2. 3 & 4 Co) working at Port Arthur 7.15 pm – 4 am. No casualties.	
March 8	Batt. warned of move tomorrow. Companies under company orders. Digging & carrying party (from various companies) working at Port Arthur 7 pm – 12 o MN.	

Time	Summary of events &c	Refs. to other papers.
arch	Day devoted to lightening of kits (superfluous kit being sent to store at La Couture.) Inspection - by companies - of rifles, emergency rations &c., and all arrangements for immediate action made	
arch 10. h - 13	(see folios ~~56 59 61 63 65 69 attached~~ 90. 91. 92 & 93	
rch 13 9 pm	Arrived La TOMO WILLOT after a march greatly delayed by blocks on the road & constant traffic. The Batt was halted for an hour at the Vieille Chapelle cross roads on this account	
arch 14	Sunday. Batt resting & cleaning up. Church parade at 3 o'clock.	
March 15 9.30am	Batt inspected by Div. General ~~Sir James Willcox~~ Anderson & Brig. General Jacobs Remainder of day devoted to cleaning up, refitting & making good deficiencies.	

30

Date	Summary of Events	Refs to App.
10/3/15	3 am. Batt moved from billets in Vieille Chapelle to positions in redoubts in Sq M 32 C.a.	
7.30 am	Artillery Bombardment by our guns of enemy position round Port Arthur & Neuve Chapelle begins.	
12 Noon	Batt moved to redoubts A1 & D7 in S 3 Cd	
2 pm	A shell burst on redoubt A1 causing 17 casualties including Major Robertson, mortally wounded.	
4.20 pm	Batt received orders to advance to Neuve Chapelle & support 2nd & 9th Gurkhas in attack on Bois de Biez right ½ Batt supporting 9th on right and left ½ Batt 2nd Gurkhas on left. Progress was extremely slow, owing to the congestion on roads caused by parties with wounded, ammunition &c. Position at 6 pm & 7 pm was approximately as shown in margin	Bois de Biez 150 yds No 2 Co. No 1 Co. 250 River Layes No 3 Co BHQ No 4 Co. near Port Arthur with prisoners greatly delayed
7 p.m.	Acting under orders, Batt withdrew over River Layes to a line about 200ʸ S.E. of road in S 5 A facing S.E. Companies proceeded to dig themselves in	

Date	Summary of Events Etc
10/3/15 11 pm.	Ration parties left about 11 pm and returned at about 2 am.
11/3/15	6 am Orders received to renew attack on Bois de Biez at 7.30 am in similar manner as detailed for previous day.
7.30 am	C.O. wounded. Adj. reports to Major Cuthbert who assumes command. Very heavy hostile fire with little artillery support and no infantry support on left makes progress difficult. O.C. 9th Gurkhas is met returning to BHQ to report situation. Orders received later to stand fast until 24th Brigade come up on our left when the attack must push on.
10 am to 2 pm.	Rifle, M.G. & artillery fire mainly directed at supports encourages Batt. to dig in.
2 pm	Very heavy fire from our batteries opened on Bois de Biez
2.15 pm	Verbal message received "Attack commences at 2.15 pm." Messages sent to O.C. R & L ½ Batts. to keep a keen look out to front and to advance at their own discretion. [Observation to the front was extremely difficult owing to the lie of the ground: nothing could be seen in the space intervening between trench W. of Rue Layes & Bois de Biez.
2.30 pm	Leading support Cos. advanced, reinforcing the Gurkhas in trench just W. of Rue Layes.

Date	Summary of Events &c.	App. &c.
11/3/15	Casualties during early part of advance were heavy:- 2 off. killed, 4 wounded, 140 other ranks.	
4 pm.	About 4 p.m. situation was as shewn in margin. Situation was discussed with 9th Gurkhas & it was decided that should the advance continue to the edge of the wood it could be done in about 3 rushes: however as our left flank was exposed owing to the non arrival of the 24th Brigade, Brigade was informed of situation, and orders were received to stand by.	400 y. River Layes Trench 2nd Gurkhas 1 Co. 4th Sea. Hrs. 9th Gurkhas 2 Cos. 4th Sea H 200 y. 1 Co. 4th Sea Hrs. Rear Trenches Road RHQ
6 pm to 2 am	Batt remained in same position until ordered to withdraw at 6 pm. & form up at S 5 a 2.5. Here Batt. remained till 2 am. when they were relieved by 1st Batt H.L.I. During interval parties were busy burying dead and collecting wounded	
2 am. 12/3/15		
March 12	Batt. marched to La Couture, progress being hampered by traffic on roads. On arrival at 5 am. a hot meal was issued.	
7. am	Batt. marched to l'Epinette R7c arriving 9 am. and went in to billets.	

92

Date:	Summary of Events.	Reff. to App
Mch 12 4[illegible] pm	Orders received to return to Richebourg. Batt moved off at 5 pm. Traffic on the roads was very heavy indeed, and the march greatly impeded, so much so that the Batt did not reach Richebourg till 10 pm; when they went into billets	
Mch 13.	Batt remained in readiness at Richebourg, until orders received to leave. Fatigue parties were detailed to go up to Neuve Chapelle to collect casualties kits etc but these had to be cancelled owing to heavy enemy artillery fire in that neighbourhood. Batt left Richebourg at 4.45 p.m.	

93

Date	Summary of Events & Information	Ref. to Appendices &c.
March 16	Muster Parade of Batt. at 3 p.m. For remainder of day companies under company arrangements for close order and extended drill, and making good deficiencies	
March 17	Batt inspected at 11.45 A.M. by Corps Comm. General Sir James Wilcocks. Strength on parade 540 men & 22 offic[rs]. Companies under their officers for drill &c 2 pm – 4 pm.	
March 18.	Companies taken in rotation by the Med. Staff for disinfecting clothes and eliminating vermin. Companies not under medical inspection paraded 10.30 – 12 M'day for extended order drill & route marching. Issue of new clothing &c during afternoon.	
March 19	Companies under company arrangements for drill, route marches &c 10.30 am to 12-30 & 2 pm - 3 pm.	
March 20.	ditto. ditto.	

31

Date	Summary of Events & Information	Ref. to App.
March 21.	Batt. Church Parade at 11 A.M. Services for Episcopalians at Locon 8 a.m. and 6 p.m.	
March 22.	Companies paraded for 3 hours drill & route marching. Batt. paraded at 2 p.m. to hear order received from Col. Macfarlane and congratulatory letter from Seaforth.	
March 23.	Companies inspected by Major Fraser. A draft of 128 men (no officers) arrived at 1 p.m. having been met at Lillers by 2nd Lt. Raillton. Orders received to move tomorrow. Afternoon spent apportioning draft to companies, packing up superfluous kit &c.	
March 24	Batt. moved at 7 o'clock (at the head of the Brigade) and marched to Bout de Ville, arriving about 8.30 a.m. Lay in an orchard there till 7 p.m. when we marched to billets round M 27 d, No. 1 & 2 Cos. being in billets close to the Estaires La Bassée Road & 3 & 4 on a cross road further back.	

32

Date	Summary of Events &c.	Ref to App
March 25	A grey misty day & consequently no shellfire till the sky cleared in the afternoon. Co. busy strengthening billets & constructing shrapnel proof dugouts. Drill for draft, 2 hours. O.C. Co & senior officers went up after dusk to see our section of firing line.	
Mch 26.	Co. engaged on dug-outs and collecting equipment, rifles &c left round billets by other units. Some shelling took place on the E – La B. road about 200 yards to S. of our H.Q. Nos 1 & 2 Co. furnished parties at night for digging near firing line & burying dead. They moved back during night to new billets at M 31 b 4.6.	
Mch 27.	Co at work as before. Some shelling again during the day but our billets were immune. Drill for draft. Foot & Rifle inspections &c	
Mch 28	Capt Ferguson, 2Lt: Macleod, Hills & Cartwright joined the Batt. Batt moved up to the firing line at 8 pm	

33

Date.	Summary of Events &c	Refs to App
28/3/15	and relieved 1st Seaforths. No 1 & 2 Cos occupied the firing line; 50 men of No 4 Co. held an advanced position in front of a ruined farm at road junction M 35 b 9.2; remainder of No 4 Co & No 3 Co. occupied support trenches and the reserve was supplied by 1 Company of the 1st Batt 9th Gurkha Rifles on our left (the trench being continuous on this flank) and on our right by the 4th (T.B) Royal Welsh Fusiliers - the latter being separated by the road on our extreme right. Very quiet night, little firing on either side. Cos in firing line busy improving fire trench, the back parapet of which is very inadequate.	
29/3/15	Firing line stood to arms 4 am - 5.30 am. Quiet day and little firing. Fine day but sharp frost at night. Cos busy improving trench, constructing dug outs, latrines &c and putting out more wire entanglements. Enemy's rifle fire became more active at 10.30 pm.: machine gun fire was also opened, and the O.C firing line stood Cos. to	

Date	Summary of Events &c	Refs to App
29/3/15	arms from 11 pm - to 12 midt., when the fire quieted down. Very cold again at night, 4 or 5° of frost.	
30/3/15	Stood to arms 4 am till 5.30 am. Firing line quiet during early morning. At 11 30 am. officer in charge of Brig Bomb mortars fired 3 rounds at suspected M.G. emplacement in trench on our left front, and 4 rounds at ruined house (suspected of harbouring snipers) on our right front. Enemy replied with 6 rounds of shrapnel just over F.T. which did no damage. We had one or two casualties during the day from rifle-fire. Evening quiet till 11 50 pm when Germans by means of an incendiary rocket set fire to the ruined farm house in our advanced post: during the fire (which was continued up till 2 am. through another small barn catching fire)	
31/3/15	the enemy kept up a hot fire from rifles & machine-guns, but no casualties resulted. During the fire the Co in the firing line and 50 men from No 3 Co, who had come up as a working party to deepen the communication trench leading from the F.L. to the post, stood to arms. One man in the working party was	

Date	Summary of [illegible]	Refs to App.
31/3/15	slightly wounded by a stray bullet. The fire did not damage the defences nor effect the position of the advanced post in any way, and was helpful in destroying débris, unburied dead &c. ~~Bn~~ Stood to arms again 4 am to 5.15 am. The morning passed quietly on both sides. About 3.30 pm the enemy fired several rounds of h.e. shrapnel at ranges varying between our support & fire trenches. At 7 pm. our bomb gunners fired effectively at the sniper's houses on our left front, and the enemy replied with six rounds of h.e. shrapnel at our fire trench and caused two minor casualties.	
	The Batt. was relieved at 9 p.m by the Connaught Rangers (3 Cos.) & 1 Co of the 4th London Regt. Companies marched back independently to billets E. of Vieille Chapelle, arriving there about ~~[illegible] pm~~ midnight.	
	Casualties during these four days in the firing line were: – Officers _ Nil: Rank & File _ Killed 2 Died of Wounds 1, Wounded 12	

Meerut Division

4th Seaforth Highlanders

From 1st To 30th April 1915

121/5504

Serial No. ~~260~~ 261

WAR DIARY

OF

4th Seaforth Highlanders.

From 1st April 1915 To 30th April 1915

H.S. 9 Meek

No BM.6
14-4-16.

App "Q"

D E H R A D U N B R I G A D E

SCHEME FOR THE DEFENCE OF SECTION TAKEN OVER on 11th/12th APRIL.

1. The main principles of the defence are as follows:-

(a). The first line of trenches must be maintained at all costs.

(b). If any part of the line is broken and occupied by the enemy, the remainder of the line will still be held.

(c). If any part of the line is broken, a local counter-attack will be delivered at once to regain the original position.

(d). In the event of an attack the Battalion in Reserve will move up to the second line defence ready both to block any gap made by the enemy and to assist in case a Local counter attack is hung up.

2. The Section is divided into four Subsections each held by a Battalion which has two Companies in the firing line and two in Local Reserve. In each Section area there is a Redoubt or Keep.

3. The co-operation of the guns should ensure that only the original attackers get anywhere near our trenches. The firing line should therefore only have to deal with an unsupported attack.

4. Should however, any of the attackers gain a footing in our trenches they must be counter attacked as soon as possible by the Local Reserves before they have time to establish themselves. With this object in view obstacles have been erected in some places behind our trenches, especially in front of NEUVE CHAPELLE, . It is considered that these obstacles will prevent the enemy gaining easy access into the ruined houses whence it would be difficult to dislodge them and also draw them off on either flank where they would come under fire of three of the Keeps. (HILL's - CHURCH - CHATEAU).

5. The Reserve Battalion would move up to the Breastwork, 2nd line Defence, now in course of construction.

6. Officers Commanding Battalions will draw up plans of action and discuss them with the Brigadier when he visits them.

[signature] Walker

Major.

Brigade Major Dehra Dun Brigade.

1/4 Seaforth Highlanders

Date.	Summary of Events &c
April 1.	Batt. resting all morning. At 4 p.m. marched to Croix Marmuse and billeted there. Found billets very close, and had great difficulty in finding shelter for the whole Batt:- e.g. the Transport drivers had to bivouac in their park.
2/4/15	Orderly Room 12 Noon. Cos. under Co. arrangements for washing, cleaning equipment &c
3/4/15	Rain hindered parades. Cos. continued cleaning & refitting
4/4/15	Church Parade 11.30 am.
5/4/15	Very heavy rain stopped parades. Cos. completed refit.
6/4/15	Cos. paraded for close order drill &c. Dental cases taken to Bethune for treatment.
7/4/15	ditto ditto.
8/4/15	Cos. paraded for drill (C.O.C.) & route marching (2 hours)
9/4/15	do during morning. Brigade inspection by G.O.C. in chief (Field Marshal Sir John French) at 3 p.m. at Lestrem; was, owing to heavy rain deferred till the
10/4/15	when it took place as arranged for the previous day.

37

Date	Summary of Events	Notes: Refs. &c.
11/4/15	Church Parade at 11.30. Senior off & all O.C. Co. away during day to reconnoitre part of line in front of Neuve Chapelle, from Brewery road 400 yards to right flank. Left half Batt marched at 6.45 remainder at ~~8~~ 7.15 by Zelobes, Vieille Chapelle & Bout de Ville to Pont Logy Rail Tail. No 3 & No 4 Co relieved two Cos of the 2nd Sussex in the firing line: No 5 Platoon relieved North Lancs in Hill's Redoubt: remaining Platoons of No 2 Co and No 1 Co relieved North Lancs in Support trenches. Relief greatly delayed by traffic on roads & pathways and relief not completed till midnight.	
12/4/15	A quiet day: except for artillery: fire re-adjusted and direct telephone communication established between fire trench and headquarters. Some 1000 Sandbags put in parapet at night.	
13th	Shelling again active. General improvements to parapets.	

Date	Summary of Events	Notes: Reff: Etc
14/4/15	Quiet day. Germans sent a fair number of small shell into old trenches behind of our No 3 Co, and between willows & Hill Redoubt. No 5 Platoon garrisoning that redoubt was relieved this evening at 8 pm by 2/2 Ghurkas.	
15/4/15	Quiet day with occasional artillery fire at various targets. During the night while directing the construction of improvements in the Listening Post (in front of our right Co.) 2nd Lt. G. M. Fitzroy was shot through the heart and died almost immediately	
16/4/15	A quiet day, as usual, and as usual the situation unchanged.	
17/4/15	Enemy batteries shelled our front line of support trenches at 10 a.m. and slightly wounded 2 men. Day otherwise quiet. Nos 1 & 2 Cos. relieved Nos 3 & 4 in the firing line. Relief completed by 11 pm.	

48

Date	Summary of Events	Refs: notes &c
18/4/15	A good deal of rifle fire during night & up to 5 a.m. Thereafter a very quiet day, little shell & less rifle fire. A German biplane flew very high down our line at 11 am. and evoked a zealous waste of S.A.A.	
19/4/15	Heavy rifle fire from Bareilly Brig. on our left during night. Stood to arms as usual 3.30 – 4.45 am & for 45 mins after sunset. Our battery registering on German trench fired 6 rounds at 6.45 am. At 8.15 am enemy shelled the Brewery and made good practise. Some h.e. shrapnel fired near trench of 1/9th Gurkhas on our left. German biplane flying very high observed for their guns 8.25 – 8.35 and then flew off N.E. Our batteries fired at long ranges over the B. de Biez during afternoon. Germans very quiet at night & no flares sent up. Patrols sent out reported working parties in & behind German lines	
20/4/15	Very quiet day. Work done improving & heightening parados making dug outs behind instead of in front of parados &c. To make good a shortage of sandbags parties were sent out at dusk to collect these from old trenches. Occasional shelling from both sides during day. Enemy biplane flew down our line at 4 pm & was duly fusilladed.	

Date Summary of Events Notes: Ref. sic

21/4/15 During night enemy rifles were very silent, while Batt. kept up a vigorous fire to harass working parties in enemies lines. About 5 a.m. enemy fired Rifle Grenades at listening post in front of No 1 Co.: one lucky shot landed in the Comm. trench (to which the post had retired) killing 1 man, mortally wounding another and wounding 3 others. Our bomb mortars replied on enemy trench & silenced them. Enemy heavy batteries shelled the Brewery again at 9 a.m. and made further marked destructural alterations in that much-abused edifice: they also fired into other houses in the village behind & S.W. of Brewery: two of these caught fire & burnt out. During the conflagration enemy sent several shortrange shrapnel shells above our trench obviously with intent to catch any too-curious spectators of the blaze: in this they followed the lead of our field battery which had burst a salvo of shrapnel above the German trench during their bombardment of the Brewery. Afternoon very quiet. Enemies attacked No 1 Co's sector again with rifle-grenades and were again silenced by our bomb mortars at 10.30 pm

22/4/15 At 3-15 a.m. an organized Hun-harassment was executed by the Bareilly Brigade on our left, who fired a vigorous 10 mins. rapid

Date	Summary of Events	Notes & Refs. &c
22/4/15	which was followed by some score rounds of shrapnel from our batteries on the enemy support & reserve trenches, the manning of which was presumed as a result of the rifle fire. The Huns betrayed their alarm by a perfect galaxy of star shells. This matutinal demonstration seems to have exhausted the energies of both sides, as the day passed even more tranquilly than usual – if possible.	
23/4/15	The enemy very quiet along our front today, but very heavy firing was heard far away to the N. Owing to the present dry sunny weather the clay of the trench works has begun to be very friable and repairs are frequently necessary: in No 2 sector several traverses have been taken down & wholly rebuilt with sandbags, work being possible both by night and day.	
24/4/15	Quiet day. Enemy shelled the Brewery again at 3 pm. No 1 Co were relieved by No 3 Co at 9 pm. and No 2 Co (with the exception of two platoons) by 2 platoons of No 4 Co. after the first relief had been effected.	

Date	Summary of Events	Notes, Refs: &c
25/4/14.	Quiet Day. Our two platoons of No 4 relieved No 2 in firing line **Draft arrived at Vieille Chapelle consisting of 13 wounded & 12 sick returned from hospital &c 81 new men from Bedford.**	
26/4/14	Very quiet day. Enemy shelled the Brewery & houses near at 6.30 pm causing the customary dissemination of bricks and splinters. Some shelling behind the lines near supports.	
27/4/14	Quiet day. Enemy shelled our support trenches – no casualties Batt relieved at 8.30 pm by 39th Gharwal Rifles. Marched to billets between the cross roads at Les 8 Maisons & Vieille Chapelle.	
28/4/14	Washing, cleaning up (and resting) greatly facilitated by brilliant summer weather: these facilities were very thoroughly employed. Owing to some confusion of Billeting Areas the Batt had to move again during the evening to billets nearer Vieille Chapelle: as the new billets were not assigned till nearly 9 pm and it was impossible to get billets for all the Companies only No 1 & 4 were moved tonight	
29/4/14	Washing & refitting continued. No 2 Co moved in the evening to new billets in Vieille Chapelle: as it was impossible to find accommodation in the very limited area assigned for No 3 Co. they were allowed – thanks to the courtesy of the O.C. 2nd Batt Black Watch – to remain in their old billets, which is properly within the Bareilly Brig. area.	

Date	Summary of Events	Notes. Reffs.
30/4/14	Companies completed cleaning up, refitting &c	

Meerut Division

1/4th Seaforth Highlanders

April 30th To June 1st 1915

Dehra Dun
Meerut

War Diary.

1/4th Seaforth Hdrs.

May 1915

DATE.	SUMMARY OF EVENTS	NOTES, REFS, etc.
April 30th	Machineguns were relieved by those of 39th Garhwals. Companies completed cleaning up, refitting, etc. Maj. J.W. Cuthbert has been awarded the Distinguished Service Order. The following have been awarded the Distinguished Conduct Medal:— Sgt. Maclennan, Pte. W.C. Minchin,.. The Battn. was issued with Balmoral bonnets with khaki covers. The change in the appearance of the men is great, ~~and the~~ the variety of headgear before having been very noticeable.	
May 1st.	The battn. was turned out at 5am. owing to a German bombardment. But nothing came of it, our guns evidently effectually replying to the fire of the Huns.	

DATE.	SUMMARY OF EVENTS	NOTES, REFS, ETC.
	An exciting incident occurred about 8.30 pm The farm occupied by C Coy went on fire. The farm itself was completely gutted out, but most of the outhouses, live-stock, etc and the dwelling-house were saved. Parties came from 2/2nd Gurkhas, 2nd Black Watch, R.F.A., & R.M.A.	
May 2nd	Sunday. Church Parade behind HQ at 11am.	
May 3rd.	Two machine guns under Sgt. Ross relieved two guns of the 6th Jats in the Orchard, Rue du Bois.	
May 4th	At 5 pm. the C.O read a paper by Gen. Haking on the attack in trench warfare. All officers, S.M's, Q.M.Rs Sgts, & Platoon Sgts were present.	

DATE	SUMMARY OF EVENTS	NOTES, REFS, ETC
May 4th	Appointments: Maj. J.W. Fraser appointed D.A.Q.M.G. at Calais. Capt. D.A. Mackenzie appointed A.M.L.O. at Calais.	
May 5th	Coy. inspections; No. 1 at 10.30am & the others at hour intervals. C.O. & Mr. Dewar went up to Ruedu Bois in forenoon. Gen. Ross, Highland Divn. paid a visit in afternoon. At 7.0pm. No. 1 coy with C coy & two remaining machine guns went to Ruedu Bois; position on left of 6th Jats, who are in the orchard.	
May 6th	In Trenches Heavy shelling by both sides throughout the day. Two guns were relieved by 2/2nd	

DATE	SUMMARY OF EVENTS	NOTES, REFS, ETC.
	& Gurkhas, but remained in trenches. At Vieille Chapelle. Coy. drill in morning & afternoon.	
May 7th	In trenches. Two casualties in No. 1 Coy soon after dawn. Heavy shelling again. Adjt. came up about 5 pm & explained plan of attack to come off on 9th. in co-operation with the French at Arras. In Vieille Chapelle. Gen. Jacob explained the attack to officers & Sgts. He was very optimistic.	
May 8th	Very little shell-fire. Heavy firing from south was heard about noon. Battn. left Vieille Chapelle about 8 pm and reached trenches about 11 pm. Nos. 1, 2 + 3 were in front line, 4 in support.	

DATE	SUMMARY OF EVENTS	NOTES, REFS, ETC.
May 9th	Sunday. [vide] Battn. billetted near Riez Bailleul.	
May 10th	Battn. mustered parade at 11am From "London Gazette":– Sec. Lieuts. to be temp. Capts.– William S. Dewar; Lionel D. Henderson; Michael G. Fitz Roy (since killed in action): dated March 15th 1915. Sec. Lieuts. to be temp. Lieuts.– Peter B. MacIntyre, Ronald R. M. Macdonald, Arthur J. Railton, Andrew K. Fraser, Arthur H. C. Hope, Mark Tennant, Charles G. Tennant: dated Nov. 1st, 1915. About 30 of our sick, etc. returned to us from Rouen; a new officer – 2nd Lt. C.H. Harris, to No 2 Coy.	

DATE	SUMMARY OF EVENTS	NOTES, REFS, ETC.
May 11th	Bde. moved to Vieille Chapelle, 1/4 Seaforths leaving Riez Bailleul at 3.0 pm. Billets round X roads R.28 D	
May 12th	Indents, cleaning, washing, etc. Lts. Gray & Hills returned from a machine gun course at St Omer.	
May 13th	Raining. Coy. rifle inspections etc.	
May 14th	Nil.	
May 15th	Battn. muster parade at H.Q. at 10 am. Burial of Lieut. Arthur Temple Railton in the cemetery at 12.30 pm. Coy Route marches. 8 pm. roll call by coys. in billets.	

DATE	SUMMARY OF EVENTS.	NOTES, REFS, ETC.
May 16th	Sunday. Battn. stood to arms at 5am. in billets. Heavy gun fire. Battn. put on 20 mins notice.	
May 17th	A wet morning.	
May 18th	Coy. route marches of 1 hour. Capt. Cameron returned from leave. Meerut Divn. moved from Vieille Chapelle to make room for our friends the Highland Divn. 1/4 Sea. left at 8.15 pm went into a very poor trench about 200 yds from the Rue du Puits between Rouge Croix & Croix Barbée. Night was wet & chilly.	
May 19th	Coys. were put into billets on Rue du Puits. A quiet day.	

DATE	SUMMARY OF EVENTS	NOTES, REFS, ETC.
May 20th	A warm day; quiet. German plane over in afternoon.	
May 21st	Another warm & quiet day. About noon a dozen large shells fell near Rouge Croix, where part of No 4 was billeted, but no one was hurt. Meerut Divn moved back to V. Chapelle, 1/4 Seaforths starting at 5pm by coys. Billets as before. The mess cart broke down near Croix Barbée, but the contents were rescued.	
May 22nd	A quiet day. A few shells came into the village but no one was hurt.	
May 23rd	Sunday C.O., O.Cs 2 & 4 coys, & M.G. went to Rue du Bois at 9am Battn Church parade at 12 noon.	

DATE	SUMMARY OF EVENTS	NOTES, REFS, ETC.
	Battn. left for trenches at 6.30 pm. Trenches in front of end of Edward Road and Factory. Nos. 1 & 2 coys were in the British line, No. 4 in ~~f~~ the extreme left of a captured German trench, & No. 3 in reserve.	GERMAN LINE BRIT. LINE
	Enemy shelled the communication trench while No. 4 was going up. Two men slightly wounded.	BRITISH LINE
May 24th	Two bombs were fired from a mortar by the enemy at nobody in particular. One burst in midair about half-way between the two lines, the other not far from No. 4.	
	A quiet day. Very little rifle fire.	
	The trenches, especially in the German lines, are very objectionable. There are numbers of dead between the two lines, & the sun has had a marked effect on them. At times the smell was well-nigh	

DATE	SUMMARY OF EVENTS	NOTES, REFS. ETC.
	unbearable. About 7.40 pm Lieut. Daman was shot through the head and killed almost at once. A great loss to us all. In No 4 coy's trench there were two alarms of gas during the night 24/25th. A pillar of smoke was seen to rise rapidly from the enemy's trench to a height of about 10 ft or more & then it spread along the ground. But in each case the wind blew the smoke away. As very little was let off, it may have been ~~used~~ to test the wind. Anyhow it gave everyone a bad fright. Between 9 & 10 pm a couple of shells burst over our listening post (No 4 coy) & wounded one man in the leg.	
May 25th	A fairly quiet day. No wind, & consequently plenty of smells.	

DATE.	SUMMARY OF EVENTS.	NOTES, REFS, ETC.
	No. 3 coy. relieved No. 4 in the advanced trench; No. 4 retired to reserve lines.	An interesting fact was brought to light by the enemy's shelling in the afternoon. They sent a few "pip-squeaks" into their trench close to our listening post; whereupon those inside sent up flares, though in full day-light, which had the effect of stopping the fire and making it change on to another part of trench.
May 26th	A fairly quiet day. A British aeroplane was forced to descend, fortunately within our lines. About 9pm 1st. Seaforths relieved 1/4th Seaforths in firing line. 1/4ths retired to Windy Corner neighbourhood	
May 27th	Enemy sent some big shells close to No. 4 coy's dug-out ~~near~~ between Lansdowne & Windy Corner. Two men were wounded in the evening by shrapnel; they belonged to No. 1 coy	
May 28th	Divn. "crocks" parade at Vieille Chapelle. "Crocks" returned after examination. A fairly quiet day.	

DATE	SUMMARY OF EVENTS	NOTES, REFS, ETC.
	A large working party was out under Capt Hogg.	
May 29th.	A fairly quiet day. Very little shelling	
May 30th	Sunday Another quiet day	
May 31st	At 1 and 3 a.m. two attempts at a bombardment were made by our artillery, lasting each a quarter of an hour. In the evening a number of shells fell round Windy Corner, but no one was hurt. Connaught Rangers relieved 1/4 Seaforths, who moved to dug-outs along Albert Rd.	
June 1st.	A pretty quiet day. A carrying party of 60 men from No. 4 under Lieut. Hope.	

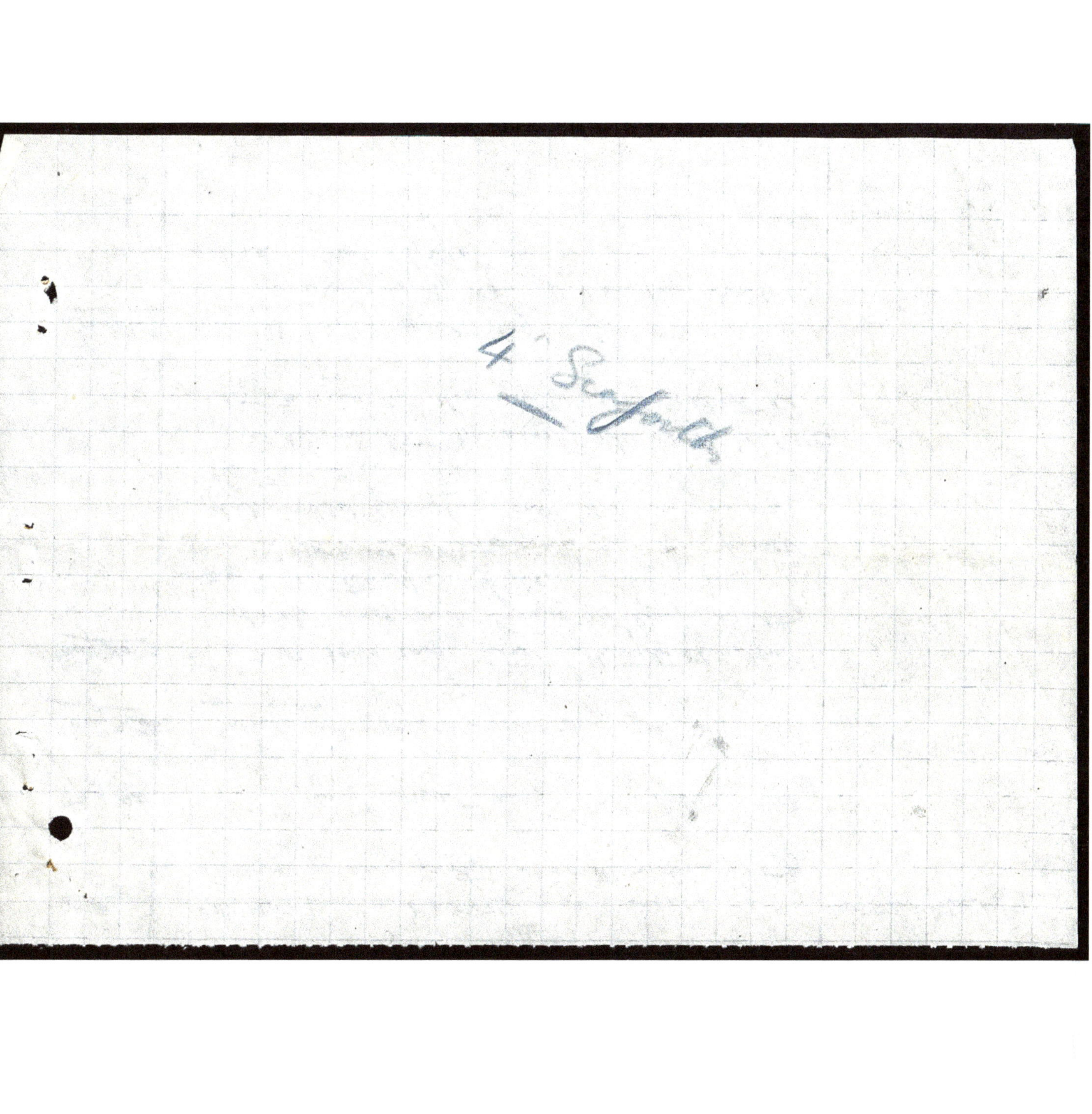
4th Seaforths

8

Meerut Division

1/4th Seafonth Highlanders

From 1st June. To July 3rd 1915

Serial No. 261.

121/2166

WAR DIARY

OF

1/4th Seaforth Highlanders

From 1st June 1915 To 30th June 1915.

6.S.
11 sheets

DATE	SUMMARY OF EVENTS.	NOTES, REFS, ETC.
June 2nd.	A quiet day on the whole. Coy. S.M. Mackenzie, No. 3, was wounded by shrapnel in the leg. About 9 pm 1/4 Seaforths relieved 6th Jats in trenches in front of Albert Road, nos. 1, 2, & 3 coys. in the firing line, no 4 in reserve A quiet night	These trenches
June 3rd.	A quiet day. Little firing on both sides	
June 4th	Another fairly quiet day. A few shells landed near the trenches, & knocked in the parapet in one or two places. A small attack was carried out on our right, but it did not develope.	

DATE.	SUMMARY OF EVENTS	NOTES, REFS etc.
June 5th	A peaceful day. German aeroplanes were active in early morning & afternoon.	
June 6th	Sunday. More German 'planes. Our firing was pretty bad. Enemy shelled part of the firing line with crumps. One shell landed in No. 3 Coy's part & wounded 7 men, three pretty badly. 1st Seaforths relieved 4th Seaforths in front trenches, 4th retiring to dug-outs close to Rue St. Vaast.	
June 7th	Nothing to report. Quiet in front. Small carrying party out under Capt. Henderson.	
June 8th	Another quiet day. Warm weather.	

DATE	SUMMARY OF EVENTS	NOTES, REFS, etc.
	Dehra Dun Bde. relieved by Jullundur Bde. 3rd London Regt. relieved 1/4th Seaforths at Cour St Vaast about 8 pm. Billets between Pont Levis in Vieille Chapelle and Zelobes.	
June 9th	Cleaning up, washing etc.	Sir John Fowler went on leave for 10 days 2Lt Summers acting adjt.
June 10th	Parades as follows: early morning 6.30 am – 7.30, physical drill and handling of arms. 10.30 am route march, followed by bathing parade. 4.30 – 5.30 pm coys under Regt. S.M. At 10 am Gen. Jacob spoke to the officers & senior N.C.O.s of each coy. He congratulated us on our good work & said that for some time to come we should look for hard work & plenty of it.	

DATE	SUMMARY OF EVENTS	NOTES, REFS.
June 11th	Parades as usual. In afternoon battn. was inspected by Gen Sir James Willcocks. Battn. came away immediately after the Gen. had finished.	
June 12th	As usual. Nothing of importance to report	
June 13th	Sunday. Church parade at 10 a.m. on inspection field followed by inspection of respirators by the C.O. Baths from 2 p.m.	
June 14th	No early morning parade. Bathing and baking of kilts.	
June 15th	Parades as per programme. Lieut. Murray, 1/9th Gurkhas, gave a demonstration of rifle grenades to officers	

DATE	SUMMARY OF EVENTS	NOTES, REFS, ETC.
	A bombardment of Rue du Bois took place in the evening.	
June 16th	C.O., ~~acting~~ Adjt, O.C. coys & M.G. went to Chocolat Meniers Corner & trenches in front of Dead Cow House at 3am. Parades for batt. as usual.	
June 17th	Reveille ~~5~~ 6 am but no parades Orderly room 10am. Valises and blankets rolled by 10.30am. 25 petrol tins were collected by each coy for water, also a number of spares. 1/4 Seaforths relieved 2nd Black Watch in trenches in front of Dead Cow House, M.G. leaving 7.30 pm & coys, No 4 leading at 8 pm, ~~at~~ with 10 minute intervals. Relief was carried out pretty well.	

DATE	SUMMARY OF EVENTS	NOTES, REFS, ETC
June 18th	A quiet night followed by a quiet day. Enemy blew in part of communicating trench to right sap-head. No casualties	
	Our front trench is protected by 2 lines of coily wire and one line of chevaux de frise. Parapet good.	
	Enemy trench hardly visible above ground. To our left there is a slight rise, but there is none on our right. High grass in front.	
	A working party from 1st Seaforth	
June 19th	Night fairly quiet began a passage behind front trench but did not complete their task till the following night.	
June 19th	Nothing to report. All quiet Bombardments of German line by 4th Corps at 3.30 a.m. & British line near	

Givenchy

June 20th Sunday. A quiet morning.

In afternoon about 4pm enemy shelled support + fire trench with crumps. Not much damage and no casualties.

No. 4 + ½ No 2 were relieved by No. 3 + ½ No. 2.

Capt. Cameron went to fire trench from reserve, Mr. Macleod to supports from reserve, + Mr. Hope to reserve from fire trench.

Capt. + Adjt. Sir John Fowler returned from leave.

June 21st A few pip squeaks over reserve in early morning.

One man killed in fire trench in morning.

DATE	SUMMARY OF EVENTS.	NOTES, REFS, ETC.
	A few crumps round Dead Cow Ho[illegible] in afternoon & evening. And one solitary shell rather late and very near H.Q. Two feeble attempts at "harassing the Hun" were made by our R.F.A. etc at 11.30 pm and 1am. Each amounted to a salvo from three or four batteries and nothing more.	
June 22nd	About 6am a number of pip squeaks fell near H.Q. but no damage was done. About 9am enemy shelled the same place with crumps, and the second shell landed in H.Q. dug out and killed poor Fowler. About 12 noon and later in the afternoon enemy shelled us again. No other casualties. All quiet in support & fire trench	On account of the heaviness of the shelling, H.Q. was moved to behind the 6th Jat line. Improvements carried out in fire trench, dug outs, etc.

DATE	SUMMARY OF EVENTS	NOTES REFS, ETC
June 23rd	Enemy dropped shells in support trench during the day. 2 casualties. 1st Seaforths relieved 1/4th Seaforths about 11 pm The Brigade line is now lengthened, 3 battns being in together. Battn. in dugouts on King's Road. These are the same trenches we came to about Dec, 20th of last year.	
June 24th	C.O. obtained 7 days' leave for Capts. Dewar and Henderson & Lieut. Hope. A heavy thunderstorm came on about 3.30 pm.	
June 25–28th	Nothing of importance. Men kept pretty well to their billets Lieut. Macleod evacuated to hospital.	

June 28th	1/4 Seaforths relieved 1/9 Gurkhas in "A" sub-section.	
June 29th to July 2nd.	A fairly quiet time; intermittent shelling went on, while towards the end enemy brought a large minenwerfer to bear on our advanced post, which was consequently evacuated temporarily. The weather made the trenches rather uncomfortable. Few casualties.	
July 3rd	Capt. Dewar and Lieut. Hope returned from leave. Capt. Henderson did not return owing to sickness. 2/2nd Gurkhas relieved 1/4 Seaforths about 11pm. 1/4 Seaforths went back to King's Road and billeted.	Lieuts Tennant and Sherman granted 7 days' leave

Meerut Division

1/4th Seaforth Highlanders

From July 1st To 1st August 1915

Serial No. 261

121/6502

WAR DIARY OF

1/4th Seaforth Highlanders.

FROM 1st July 1915. TO 31st July 1915

7.8
11 sheets

DATE	SUMMARY OF EVENTS	NOTES, REFS, ETC.
July 4th	Sunday. Coy. Services in afternoon. 2nd Lieut Cartwright evacuated to hospital. A German aeroplane ventured over our lines but was at once driven away.	
July 5th.	Nothing of importance.	
July 6th	A draft of about 150 men from 2/4ths and 3/4ths arrived in evening. Most of them, the men from 3/4 ths, ~~—~~ are all old hands. This draft is the best we have had in every way.	
July 7th	The draft was distributed among the various coys. 1/4th Seaforths relieved 2/2nd Gurkhas in "A" subsection about 11 pm. Nos. 2 & 3 coys.	

DATE	SUMMARY OF EVENTS	NOTES, REFS &c.
	seven in the front line; no. 4 in support and no. 1 in reserve.	
July 8th	A quiet day. At night a working party from 2/2nd Gurkhas worked on Pink Rat trench from supports to reserve.	
July 9th	About stand-to arms, enemy played up on front trench with rifle grenades, while about 5 or 6 a.m. they sent over two or three heavy bombs. One of these just cleared the trench and made an enormous hole about 10 ft by 2.5 ft. In afternoon enemy shelled K.O.S.B.'s lines. A very still night. Hardly a rifle shot or flare near our front.	

DATE	SUMMARY OF EVENTS	NOTES, REFS ETC.
July 10th	About 6am enemy shelled KOSBs again but did not touch us. A very quiet day. Officers of 2nd Yorks came up to see the trenches about 1pm. 2nd Yorks relieved 1/4th Seaforths, who ~~thereupon~~ proceeded to Vieille Chapelle via [illegible] by coys. At Vieille Chapelle we marched as a battn to La Gorgue. We arrived about 3-30am Sunday	
July 11th	Sunday Nothing doing till 4:0 pm when there was an Orderly Room. Battn. church parade beside the canal at 6:0pm	
July 12th	Orderly Room 11am. Coy route marches of 1 hours in morning after O.R. Battn under C.M.R. Glass at 3pm for drill. At same hour bombers under Lt. Hope, signallers under Mr Summers, & Maxim Gun under Lt. Hills.	

DATE	SUMMARY OF EVENTS	NOTES, REFS, ETC.
July 13th	C.O., O.C. coys & M.gun to trenches at 9am in front of Neuve Chapelle, to posit on the right of our position there in April. Payed out companies. Bathing at La Gorgue by coys. at 7.30 am Concert was held on church parade field at 6pm. Several of 1st Sea. officers & men were present. Three Generals honoured the proceedings with their presence, viz. Gen. Bannatyne Allason and Gen Ross (Highland Divn) and Gen. Strickland (Jullundur Bde). The Motor Ambulance Corps provided several excellent "turns".	
July 14th.	Orderly Room 10am. New officers arrived from Fort George under Maj. Monro & Allan and were distributed to companies as margin. Battn. paraded at HQ at 8.15 pm.	Maj. Monro. Lt. [illegible] 2nd Lt. R.W. Hislop " J.S. Harris.

DATE	SUMMARY OF EVENTS	NOTES, REFS, ETC.
	order 4, 1, 2, 3, and marched to Euston Post via Estaires – La Bassée road. At Euston Post nos 4 & 1 met guides for front line & proceeded up the railway to Neuve Chapelle, & then to front trenches via Hill's Redoubt. Nos. 2 & 3 went on to billets between Euston Post and Port Logy. The night was the worst we have experienced since winter, the rain & mud soaking everyone. Added to the pitch darkness of the night, the coys for fire trench had a very rough time getting up to their positions. Relief was complete about 2am next day.	The new officers are :– Maj. Munro; Lt. C. W. R. Finch; 2nd Lt. Leslie Vickers; " T. Thomson; " J. [illegible]; " J. [illegible]; " [illegible]; " J. [illegible]; " W. S. Evans; " R. W. Hislop; " J. S. Harris
July 15th	Day was fortunately dry, and we managed to clean the trenches pretty well. About 11am enemy pip squeaked front line. No casualties or damage.	

DATE	SUMMARY OF EVENTS	NOTES, REFS, etc.
	Enemy was quiet all day.	
	At 9 pm a patrol went out under Lt Peverell. ~~[illegible]~~	
	Night quiet.	
~~July~~	Working done on communication trenches etc. Grass was cut in front by no. 4 coy	
July 16th	A quiet day on the whole. Enemy shelled front line with pip squeaks landing two hits on right of no 4 coy, & cutting down a tree	
	Patrol went out from No 4 coy under Lt. Peverell. Reported enemy working on wire, also a sound of wheels as of trolleys or wheelbarrows. Also heard enemy pulling down a house.	
July 17th	~~[illegible]~~ Quiet again; as usual enemy shelled front line	

DATE	SUMMARY OF EVENTS	NOTES, REFS, ETC.
July 18th	Sunday. By way of a change, front trenches were shelled about noon and not in the afternoon. Enemy dropped two or three pip squeaks on reserve coys' billets.	
July 19th	All quiet except usual shelling. Two slight casualties in front line and one in our maxim gun section.	
July 20th	By way of answering a demonstration of last night in which 1st Seaforths took part, enemy crumped their right, killing two and wounding a few men. Another three slight casualties in front line in forenoon, which were succeeded by four more in afternoon from one pip squeak all quite slight.	

DATE	SUMMARY OF EVENTS	REFS, NOTES, ETC.
	Capt. Forsyth went to hospital, Capt Hogg taking command of front line	
July 21st	Front line ~~[illegible]~~ escaped shelling till evening, when he fired on us because we were shooting at his aeroplanes. What damage we did to ~~them~~ we cannot say, but ~~they~~ did not venture very close to us. ~~Later~~ it was reported from 1st Seaforths ~~that~~ one was brought down, but ~~[illegible]~~ one of our own came over at ~~the time~~. A patrol from No 1 met an enemy patrol and retired before it.	Extract from "London Gazette", July 21st:— Lieuts. to be temp. Capts: A.H.C. Hope April 11th. M. Lennard May 6th. 2nd Lieuts to be temp. Lieuts:— H. J. Cartwright, & C. H. Harris, April 11th, C.A.P. Hills, May 24th, C.B. Sherman, June 9th. Date of appt as qmr. & hon. Lieut. of J. Glass is March 11th not as in "Gazette" of June 22nd
July 22nd.	Front line was pip-squeaked from 9.45 – 10.45 a.m. 47th Sikhs relieved ~~the 1st Seaforths~~ in firing line about 11 p.m. The night was wet and muddy, and it must	

DATE	SUMMARY OF EVENTS	NOTES, REFS, ETC.
	very unpleasant for the Indians, especially as ~~they~~ the coys which relieved nos. 1 & 4 were all new men.	
July 23rd	No. 4 got to Pont du Hem about 2 am, no. 1 coming an hour later. Capt. Henderson came back from extended leave, Lt. Summers ~~returning~~ at the same time. Lt. Gray has an extension. Our new battn. Sergt. Major has come. S.M. Anderson, an ex-guardsman, who was instructor to a coy. of 6th Seaforths. A very fine man. Capt. Hogg went to hospital.	
July 24th	Nothing of interest.	
July 25th	Sunday ~~[illegible]~~ C.O. inspected nos 1 & 4 coys at Pont du Hem in afternoon.	

DATE	SUMMARY of EVENTS	NOTES, REFS, etc.
July [illegible]	Nos. 1 & 4 relieved Nos. 2 & 3 at Port Logy	
July 27th.	Capt. Hyde, Mr. J. Harris and 50 men as garrison to Curzon Post.	
July 28th – July 31st	Nothing of importance. Working begun at Curzon Post by the garrison.	
~~July~~ July 31st	1/4th Seaforths relieved at Port du Hem & Port Logy by 1/4th London Regt. Battn. proceeded to billets in La Gorgue.	
Aug 1st.	Sunday Church Parade 5 pm. Maj. Macneil (1st Seaforths padre) preached the sermon.	

Meerut Division

1/4 Seaforth Highlanders

From 1st August, To 1st Sept 1915

Serial No. 261.

1/6958.

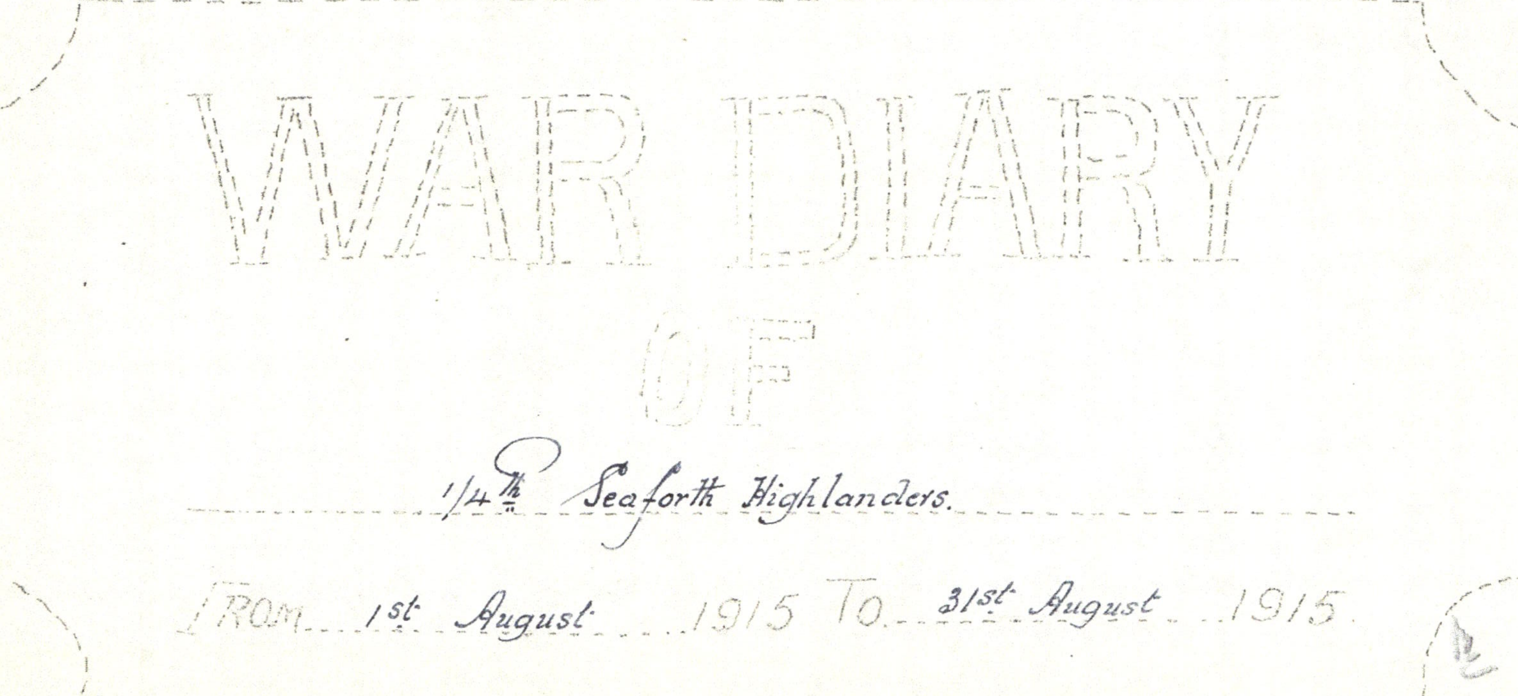

WAR DIARY

OF

1/4th Seaforth Highlanders.

FROM 1st August 1915 TO 31st August 1915.

8 S
11 sheets

DATE	SUMMARY OF EVENTS	NOTES, REF., ETC.
Aug 2nd to Aug 6th	Parades for these five days as follows:– Coy. close order drill, etc at 10 ~~30~~ am, Subalterns at 11.15 under Regtl. S.M., and all N.C.O.s at noon under S.M. From 10 – 10.30 No. 1 Coy under S.M. No. 2 under C.Q.R. [illegible], 10.30 – 11 No. 3 under S.M., No. 4 under S.M.R. Route marches in afternoon for an hour. Specialists' parades at 10.30 am	
Aug 3rd	A concert with 1st Seaforths in evening	
Aug 4th	Inter-regt. cricket match with 1st Seaforths at 2.30 pm. 1st Seaforth Officers 21 all out. 4th Officers 81 for 6. Capt Dewar made 37 for us, while Lieut Dunne was successful as a bowler. In evening [illegible] at the Corps [illegible] [illegible].	

DATE	SUMMARY OF EVENTS	NOTES, REFS, ETC.
Aug. 5th	Lt. W. Gordon 2nd Gordons, arrived to take over duties as Adjutant to our battn.	
Aug 6th	Capt. Cameron & Lt. Col. Haines on 7 days' leave. Capt. H.[illegible] to command of no 2 coy. A party of two officers and 23 men went to Ringhem, near Aire, for shooting practice with telescopic & other sights.	
Aug 7th	C.O. & O.C. coys to front line trenches in Duck's Bill section. Muster parade of battn. under Adjt at 11a.m.	
Aug 8th	Sunday Combined church parade with 1st Seaforths at 11a.m. 1/4th Seaforths relieved 2nd Gordons in Duck's Bill section. Four platoons	

DATE	SUMMARY OF EVENTS	NOTES, REFS, ETC.
	the Royal Warwickshire Regt attached as per margin for instruction for 48hrs	In right subsection, no 2 coy + 1 platoon RW. Left subsect. no 4 + 1 platoon. In Duck's Bill, ½ no 3 coy + 1 platoon – in Lafore Post ½ no. 3 + 1 platoon In reserve on Rue Tilleloy no 1 coy
Aug 9th	Night was quite quiet, but at stand to arms, enemy opened a heavy fire for about half an hour. C.O. Adjt. and C.O. Royal Warwicks came round in morning.	
Aug 10th	About 6.30 am enemy fired four bombs from a minenwerfer at Duck's Bill, one of which failed to explode. An officer + 2 men of the Warwicks and 2 of ours were wounded slightly. Our 1½" mortars replied with three bombs. Rest of the day was very quiet. 4 more platoons Royal Warwicks came up.	Subsequent examination showed the bomb to be of about 100 lbs. weight.
Aug 11th	Another quiet day. Mr. Glennan accompanied a patrol.	

DATE	SUMMARY OF EVENTS	NOTES, REFS, ETC.
Aug 11th	About 12:30 am we had a small hate at point 143 with 1½" & small mortars and rifle grenades. About 22 of the small bombs were fired. All the bombs burst but the damage was not known. A man in no 1 (reserve) coy was struck by a rocket and was killed. Enemy was seen at work at 143.	
~~Aug 13th~~	"Mother" fired 6 rounds at 197 at 4 pm.	
Aug 12th	Another peaceful night and day. At 5 pm our 4.5 hows. fired on 197. 1/9th Gurkhas sending up a red rocket at 4 pm. to give the line. 2/3rd Gurkhas relieved 1/4th Seaforths in Duck's Bill section except Lahore Post. 4th Seaforths went back to Rugby Road, Royal Warwicks leaving us at Rue Bacquerot.	

DATE	SUMMARY OF EVENTS	NOTES, REFS, &c.
Aug [illegible]	Baths at La Gorgue open to officers. One from each coy. went at a time.	— [illegible] S end of it had some 6 yds of front trench obliterated by mines earlier about 6am. Only one casualty, a sergeant shot.
Aug. 14th	Saturday OC coys warned at noon to prepare for going into trenches tonight. OC coys & Adjt. at HQ 6th Jats at 2 pm. We have 2 coys in front line nos 2 & 3; no 2 holds from MIN trench to WINCHESTER ROAD including the "Birdcage". no 3 to right of MIN. No 4 in reserve, no 1 holds two redoubts. 4 platoons 8th North Staffords in front line with us. Relieved 6th Jats about 9 30 pm.	The 6th Jats, 41st Dogras, 4th Gurkhas & 47th Sikhs are withdrawn from the Corps & are going to Egypt.
Aug 15th	Sunday A very quiet day. C.O. & Adjt. round in morning. Afternoon and evening wet.	

DATE	SUMMARY OF EVENTS	NOTES, REFS, ETC
Aug 16th.	Wet in morning. CO & Adjt. round lines again. Capt Dewar takes over from 1st Seaforths front line only; he has two platoons of N. Staffs attached to him, while only one relieve each two platoons at present with nos 2 & 3 coys.	
Aug 17th.	At 4 pm Mother (9.2 how) fired 12 rounds at point 263 opposite the Birdcage. Damage reported as considerable, though the front parapet was not much damaged. Our 4.5 hows. followed up with a number of lyddite shells, though their first shell, fortunately only shrapnel, hit the ground behind the 3rd Londons on our left.	
Aug 18th.	Gen. Jacob and an R.E. colonel visited the line today and looked at the Bird-Cage.	

DATE	SUMMARY OF EVENTS	NOTES, REFS, ETC
	No. 4 coy relieved no. 2 in Birdcage sub-section, when no. 2 moved in between nos. 1 & 3 to fill up the gap caused by the departure of the Staffords, as only 2 platoons 9th Welch Regt. relieved the coy of Staffords & were attached to nos 3 & 4. A rather unnecessary movement.	
Aug 19th	More generals visit the Birdcage. Gens. Anderson & Jacob were up today.	
	Acting on information supplied by a deserter who gave himself up to the 9th Gurkhas some days ago, our machine guns and supporting 18 prs. fired at points behind enemy lines between 8.30 & 11.30 pm in the hope of bagging reliefs etc which should have come off ~~tonight but~~ that night.	

DATE	SUMMARY OF EVENTS	NOTES, REFS etc
Aug 20th	Another quiet day, very warm too. 1st Seaforths relieved 1/4th Seaforths about 10pm; 1/4th Seaforths returned to Rugby Road.	
Aug. 21st	Baths at La Gorgue open to us. Nos. 3 & 4 went in afternoon. Carrying party from no 1 coy under Lieut Peverell.	
Aug 22nd	Baths open for nos 1 & 2 in early morning. Church parade by coys.	
Aug 23rd	Inspection of billets by C.O. commencing with no 2 coy at noon. Carrying party from no 1 & 3 under Capt. Dewar.	
Aug 24th	Some bombing in early morning was replied to vigorously by our 18 prs.	

DATE	SUMMARY OF EVENTS	NOTES, REFS, ETC.
	Relieved by 4th Black Watch, when we proceeded to billets at La Gorgue, arriving about 10 pm	
Aug 25th – Aug 28th	Orderly Room 9.30 am. The first two days were taken up with re-inoculation of those who were done before April last. A working party (75 per each day) on 28th. Cricket match v. Bde HQ. Officers and men. 1/4th Seaforths 80, Bde HQ about 30. Battn. HQ moved on 27th to [illegible] and La Gorgue – Merville owing to [illegible] coming into La Gorgue & taking over our HQ. Lieut. Harvey came back on [illegible]th. 2 Lieut. [illegible] went to England on 7 days' leave.	
Aug 29th	Sunday Church parade with 1/4 Seaforths	

DATE.	SUMMARY of EVENTS.	NOTES, REFS, etc.
	1/4th Seaforths & 2/2nd Gurkhas went out to Pont du Hem and thereabouts as advanced Div. reserve, owing to rumours of intended gas attacks. 1/4th Seaforths proceeded by coys to Pont du Hem via Riez Bailleul.	
	At Pont du Hem 1 man was killed & 14 wounded ([illegible] 5 severely) by the explosion of a Double Cylinder bomb, all these casualties being in No 1 Coy.	
	Fatigue party of 50 men per coy.	
Aug 30th	4 Coys [illegible] positions [illegible] should the enemy break through; no 1 coy Pont du Hem, no 2 [illegible] Post, no 3 [illegible], no 4 [illegible].	
Aug 31st	[illegible] battn out on fatigue tonight, digging new trench from Rue Bacquerot.	
Sept 1st	Battn out carrying party.	

Meerut Division

1/4th Seaforth Highlanders

From 1st To 30th Sept 1915

Serial No. 261.

Confidential

121/7286

War Diary

with appendicees.

of

1/4th Seaforth Highlanders.

FROM 2nd September 1915. TO 30th September 1915.

DATE	SUMMARY OF EVENTS	NOTES, REFS, ETC
	up as much as possible.	
Sept 30th.	Battn. marched by coys. to La Gorgue for baths as follows, No 3 at 9 am. No 1 at 10 am. and Nos 2 & 4 in the afternoon. More rain in evening.	
Oct. 1st.	Orderly Room 10 am. Parades and coy. inspections under coy. arrangements.	
Oct 2nd.		

DATE.	SUMMARY OF EVENTS	NOTES, REFS, ETC.

rain fell again in evening and continued all night.

Relieved in the line by a bde of the XX th Divn, 1st Seaforths coming out quite early in the day. ~~They then~~ 4th Seaforths received orders to prepare for relief at 2 pm but got no orders to move till after 6 pm. By ~~this~~ time the trenches were in a rotten ~~state~~ again and ~~the~~ it was raining really hard.

Battn proceeded by Pont Logy, Rouge Croix & Lacouture to Vieille Chapelle for billets; arrived at Lacouture to find no billets. However these were found about half an hour later. By ~~the~~ time everyone was soaked to the skin and mud to the eyes.

Sept 29th. A cold, dreary day. Spent in drying &

DATE	SUMMARY OF EVENTS	NOTES, REFS, ETC.
	brigade HQs. And they cannot have been supported properly; ~~or~~ they would not have had to fall back. There were blunders somewhere, difficult to trace to their source perhaps, but they were obvious to anyone. Anyhow, a show which might easily have been crowned with success met with defeat.	
Sept 26th	Dehra Dun Bde. holds ~~front~~ line as on 24th 1st Seaforths & 2/2nd Gurkhas being in front line; 1/4th Seaforths in B line. Everyone was pretty tired, so most of the day was spent in sleeping. ~~The~~ Trench was cleaned up and got quite decent.	
Sept 27th	Day again fine but rain came in afternoon and the trenches got bad again.	
Sept 28th	Trenches again were cleaned up but	

DATE	SUMMARY OF EVENTS	NOTES, REFS, ETC.
Sept 5th–8th	A very quiet four days. An immense amount of work was done by night and day, parties from different regiments working under R.E. at sallyports and shelters under the fire step in nearly every bay. These shelters are intended for gas cylinders. A number of new communication trenches have been and are being dug; the main communication trenches were boarded during the four days. Ammunition dug-outs, emplacements for machine guns, trench mortars and even field guns in the front line. On night 7th/8th. Lieut. Vickers was grazed on the forehead by a bullet.	
Sept 9th–10th.	1/4th Seaforths and 1/9th Gurkhas in 2 line, 1st Seaforths & 2/3rd Gurkhas in front line. Every afternoon a good deal of	

DATE	SUMMARY OF EVENTS	NOTES, REFS ETC
	gun fire on our front.	
	On afternoon 11th about 5 pm a German aeroplane was brought down by our anti-aircraft guns after only 6 shots. Hardly had the machine reached the ground when three field batteries were sending over salvoes of shell. Two or three heavies followed later on.	
Sept 12th	Sunday. ~~[illegible]~~ [illegible] Gradually relieved Dehra Dun. 1/4th Seaforths went to La Gorgue in afternoon. Same billets	
Sept 13th –17th.	The usual four days' programme, cleaning up for first two days, muster parade on 15th and inspection by C.O. with the Batt. coy. as usual. ~~[illegible]~~ Batt. baths on 16th at Corps Baths	

DATE	SUMMARY OF EVENTS	NOTES, REFS &c.
Sept 15th	Maj. Gen. Jacob, commdg. Meerut Divn, came round to say goodbye to us and ~~Lieut Gen Sir~~ good luck under our new Brigadier Col. Harvey, 2nd Black Watch.	Lieut Gen. Sir Charles Anderson now commands the Indian Corps, Gen Willcocks having got another appointment.
Sept 17th	Brig. Gen. Harvey (late Lt Col 2nd Black Watch) ~~[illegible]~~ came round at 6 pm.	
Sept 18th	Dehra Dun relieved Garhwal & Bareilly. ~~[illegible]~~ 1/4th Seaforths take from Sunken Road and Duck's Bill (inclusive) to left of South Moated Grange Street. No 2 in Duck's Bill, nos 3 & 4 as before between Sunken Road and Colvin, and no 1 on left of Colvin. O.C. coys went up early in afternoon.	
Sept 19th	Sunday A beautiful day. At 5 pm a fleet of 11 French aeroplanes, "fighter" or "Voisin" type, came	

DATE	SUMMARY OF EVENTS	NOTES, REFS, ETC.
	over our lines in a bunch. They separated when the Germans fired their first shell, and went independently over the enemy lines heading in the La Bassée direction.	
	A heavy cannonade to the south.	
Sept 20th	Nothing of much interest. The usual afternoon's shelling.	
	Enemy retaliated with small bombs and rifle grenades at South Moated Grange Street, the latter causing three casualties in a coy. 1st Sea. in support.	
	We were instructed to keep up a continuous rifle fire at nights and to fire a lot of rifle grenades.	
Sept 21st.	Guns began early today, at 5.30 am and kept up a heavy fire all day. Mortars and the 8 in. Hows very active. Some of	

DATE	SUMMARY OF EVENTS	NOTES, REFS, ETC.
	the shooting was excellent. Enemy again fired at South Moated Grange Street. Further casualties in 1st Seaforths. Rifle grenades and bombs were fired at the enemy trench mortar and silenced it. <u>Extracts from brigade orders for 22nd Sept 1915</u>: <u>1. INFORMATION.</u> 1st Army is assuming the offensive in the southern portion of the line, the Indian & other corps not engaged in the main offensive are carrying out local operations all along the 1st Army front. <u>The Indian Corps will</u>:— (a) attack the enemy's line between <u>Sunken Road</u> and <u>Winchester Road</u> and establish our line along the road running through MAUQUISSART to the DUCK'S BILL	

DATE	SUMMARY OF EVENTS	NOTES, ETC.

[Extracts from Bde orders cont.]

(b) Press on with its left in front till its left gains the high ground between HAUT POMMEREAU and LA CLIQUETERIE FERME

(c) Continue its advance from there in a south-easterly direction

The Meerut Divn. will make the attack. Lahore & XX divns. will co-operate and maintain touch when Meerut Divn advances beyond the enemy's first & second lines

2. INTENTION. The Garhwal & Bareilly Bdes will make the assault.

The Dehra Dun Bde. will be in Divisional reserve.

16. Packs. Packs will not be carried. Arrangements will be made to stack packs during night preceding assault.

DATE	SUMMARY OF EVENTS	NOTES, REFS, ETC.
	[Extracts from Bde orders contd]	
	20. GENERAL INSTRUCTIONS. The importance of advancing at all costs must be impressed on all ranks. . . .	
	It is most important that communication is kept up.	
Sept 22nd.	Gun fire as yesterday. This is the second day of the four days' bombardment preceding the assault.	
	Heavy firing from South. Probably ~~at~~ between Cuinchy and Vermelles.	
~~[illegible]~~	We are going to use gas and smoke in this attack. Lieut. Morrison has been appointed in command of ~~[illegible]~~ smoke section of 1/4th Seaforths, which consists of about 100 men from nos 3 & 4. The gas is controlled by the R.E.	

DATE	SUMMARY OF EVENTS	NOTES, REFS, ETC.
Sept 23rd.	At 6am cylinders containing asphyxiating gas were brought up and placed in the shelters under the fire steps in groups of 3 and 4 every 20 or 30 yds. The wind is not favourable at present but is expected to be on 25th. Between 6 & 10am enemy blew in a large portion of our line near Birdcage with large minenwerfers. Fortunately the gas cylinders had not been put in them. Artillery busy all day. Cannonade to south positively terrific.	
Sept 24th.	Gunfire unabated in intensity. Dull, wind not very good. About 8pm Jullundur and Bareilly Bdes took over front line. 1/4th Seaforths retired to Rouge Croix neighbourhood. At 5pm wind blew between the lines from south.	

DATE	SUMMARY OF EVENTS	NOTES, REFS, ETC.
Sept 25th	Morning broke drizzly with a very light breeze veering between SW & S. Not very favourable for gas.	
	At 5.45 a.m. the mine under pt. 263 (opposite the Bird Cage) was fired and 2 minutes after the guns began an intense bombardment, while the gas was turned on.	
	Programme was as follows:–	
	– 0.2 (ie 2 minutes before ZERO) Mine fired.	
	0.0 Daylight rocket signal sent up from Bareilly Bde. HQ.	
	0.0 Commencement of gas.	
	0.0 Artillery, except guns in front parapet open with shrapnel on enemy's front trench & HE on rear defences.	
	0.4 Two field guns in front parapet & Hotchkiss open fire.	
	0.5 Smoke screen commences on flanks.	

DATE	SUMMARY OF EVENTS	NOTES, REFS, ETC.
	Time Table cont:-	
	0.5 Smoke screen commences on entire front with the gas.	
	0.8 Gas cut off.	
	0.8 Infantry fill up all bays of fire trench and get into position to cross parapet.	
	0.9 Infantry cross parapet and form up.	
	0.9 Artillery lifts 100 yards.	
	0.9 Gun near Bird Cage ceases fire	
	0.10 Assault commences	
	0.10 Gun near Duck's Bill ceases fire.	
	0.11 Artillery lifts another 100 yds.	
	0.14 Artillery lifts to German 2nd position 500 yards in rear,	
	0.15 Smoke screen stops	
	0.20 Hotchkiss gun on parapet ceases fire	

DATE	SUMMARY OF EVENTS	NOTES, REFS, ETC.
	In this case zero was 5.45 am. Everything went all right except the gas, for the wind was too light to blow it well and blew too much from the south to send it straight over our parapet. The gas came back slightly in places and not a few men were "gassed". Both the gas and smoke travelled so slowly that the 2nd Leicesters had to get through the smoke to get into position.	
	The whole of the Bareilly Bde. went over and attacked three lines of trenches with ease and the 2/8th Gurkhas with the Leicesters' left got over all right too. But those of the Leicesters who were to assault the redoubt opposite Colvin Street (p. 147) were hung up in the enemy's wire. The 2/3rd Gurkhas got over, but their grenadiers did not support them so they got bombed and had to fall back, pretty badly	

DATE	SUMMARY OF EVENTS	NOTES, REFS, ETC.

knocked about. The 3rd Londons did not leave the Duck's Bill at all.

The Bareilly Bde. hung on for quite a long time, but was forced to fall back to its original line by nightfall.

We captured some 300 prisoners & a number of machine guns & one revolver gun in the enemy's front line, which however had to be abandoned later on.

On the left of the Meerut Divn. the XX th divn. captured four lines but were driven back again.

So our gains amount to a few prisoners, which are probably nullified by the prisoners captured by the Huns.

As to our own movements, shortly after 7 a.m. the Battn. went up Sunken Street to the B line, whence we again moved a little after 11 a.m. to the front line via Sunken St.

DATE	SUMMARY OF EVENTS	NOTES, REFS, ETC.
	and Colvin St. in order to attack pt. 197 where the Leicesters had failed. We took nearly three hours getting up the trench and even then did not reach the front line which was crowded to overflowing with troops. So we had to cram ourselves into a support trench between Colvin & South Tilleloy Streets. Here we remained from 3 pm – 7 pm. ~~and~~ in a shallow trench with no shelters, and to add to the discomfort rain fell about 4.30 pm. Fortunately the enemy had very few guns of any kind, and these he did not direct at our part of the line. The supports behind the Bird Cage seemed to get a pretty rough time.	
	About 7 pm. the battn moved back to B line by South Tilleloy Street and was put on 1 hour's notice. The trenches by this time were absolutely awful, mud up and over the ankles and in places even worse.	

DATE	SUMMARY OF EVENTS	NOTES, REFS, ETC.

Thus ended our third fight; our casualties were very few, mostly being men in the left half battn who had been slightly "gassed" in the morning.

We had a splendid chance of carrying out the first part of our intentions namely to push our line to the Mauquissart–Duck's Bill road, though the latter part of the programme was perhaps rather too much to be expected. The enemy were shaken by our bombardment and the mine and gas must have made them worse, they had very few guns and though these were used a good deal they were not nearly enough to cover the front or cause us much uncon-venience unless concentrated on one spot. But somehow things went wrong. it was probably due to faulty communication with the assaulting troops and their

Though the Indian Corps' attack failed the 1st Army's main attack to south of La Bassée canal met with gratifying success.

Great news from French at Arras & in Champagne.

DATE	SUMMARY OF EVENTS	NOTES, REFS, ETC
	Battn. grenade section began course of instruction by Bde. grenade officer at HQ. Lieut Summers went in charge of the party.	
Sept. 2nd and 3rd	Nothing of importance to note. Large carrying party with ammunition to Colvin & Lefore posts on 3rd. Very wet at first. 100,000 rounds were taken to each post.	
Sept 4th	Battn. grenadiers returned. OC coys, etc. to trenches to take over stores at 1pm at Clonegar Farm. Dehra Dun Bde relieved Bareilly from ~~S~~ Sign Post Lane to Winchester Road. 4th Seaforths relieved 69th Punjabis and 1 coy 4th Black Watch. HQ at Clonegar Farm. No. 1 coy in Duck's Bill, nos 2,3,4 from Sign Post to Sunken Road and Sunken Road to Colvin respectively.	

Secret

Operation Order 54. Copy No ....4....

by.

Lieut Colonel W. J. St. J. HARVEY.

Commanding Dehra Dun Brigade.

16th September 1915.

Reference Sheets 36 and 36a and Trench Map.

1. DEHRA DUN Brigade will relieve GARHWAL and BAREILLY Brigades in IND. 5. trenches on 18th September 1915.
2. Movements in accordance with attached table. Details to be arranged between Comdg Officers concerned.
3. The following works will be handed over to BAREILLY Brigade by 1. p m on 18th Instant. Guards now in occupation will rejoin Units:— HARROW, ETON, CHELTENHAM, PONT DU HEM. BOUT DEVILLE, CLIFTON WORKS and LA GORGUE CEMETRY.
4. Numbers 5, 11 and 13 Trench Batteries will be attached to the Brigade.
5. Reports to M. 8. d.

Issued at 8 pm.

Major
Bde Major Dehra Dun Bde

Copies 1 and 2 retained
Copy 3 to 1st Seaforths
Copy 4 to 4th Seaforths
Copy 5 to 9th Gurkhas
Copy 6 to 2nd Gurkhas
Copy 7 to Meerut Div
Copy 8 to C. R. A
Copy 9 to C. R. E
Copy 10 to Garhwal Bde
Copy 11 to Bareilly Bde
Copy 12 to 2 Coy Meerut Train
Copy 13 to Bde M. G. O
Copy 14 to Bde B. G. O
Copy 15. Bde S. O
Copy 16 Bde G. O.
Copy 17. 5 Trench Bty
Copy 18 11 Trench Bty
Copy 19 13 Trench Bty
Copy 20. 4th Cavalry.
Copy 21 Jullunder Bde

S E C R E T

Head Quarters Dehra Dun Brigade.

16th September 1915.

Copy of a memo from G.H.Q. to 1st Army No O.B.780, dated the 13th September 1915, received under Meerut Div's No. G.197, dated the 15th September 1915.

:-:-:-:-:-:-:-:-:-:-:-:

It has been brought to notice that Officers, and particularly those of the higher ranks, are in the habit of visiting Artillery Observation Stations and other important positions outside the area of the Army to which they belong, without previous reference to the Commander of the body of troops affected.

2. The importance of attracting as little attention as possible to these places is so great that the Field Marshal Commanding in Chief feels it necessary to call upon Army and Cavalry Corps Commanders to issue orders prohibiting Officers from visiting defensive positions in the zones of other Armies, except for some definite tactical purpose and with the concurrence of the Army Commander concerned.

No B.M.8.

From.

The Brigade Major

Dehra Dun Brigade.

To.

The Officer Commanding

1st Seaforth Highlanders.
4th Seaforth Highlanders.
9th Gurkha Rifles.
2nd Gurkha Rifles.

Forwarded for information and guidance.

Major.

Brigade Major Dehra Dun Brigade.

S E C R E T

Head Quarters Dehra Dun Brigade

17th September 1915.

Copy of a letter from the Brigade Major, Royal Artillery Meerut Division. To Head Quarters Dehra Dun Brigade. No 1817/R.A. (L). dated the 17th September 1915.

:-:-:-:-:-:-:-:-:-:-:-:

Reference your Operation Order No 54 re relief. Your front will be supported as follows:-

"IND.5.A" by 4th Brigade R.F.A. (less 68th Battery)- Head Quarters at M.8. central. 7th Battery on Right portion and 14th Battery on left portion.

"IND.5.B." by 13th Brigade R.F.A. - Head Quarters at M.9.c.1/3. 8th Battery on Right Portion and 44th Battery on Left Portion. 2nd Battery under control of O.C. 13th Brigade R.F.A.

In addition the 60th and 61st/Howitzer Batteries are in action on the front of "IND.5" under the immediate orders of MEERUT Divisional Artillery.

No B.M. 7.

From.

The Brigade Major

Dehra Dun Brigade.

To.

The Officer Commanding

1st Seaforth Highlanders.
4th Seaforth Highlanders.
9th Gurkha Rifles.
2nd Gurkha Rifles.

Forwarded for information.

Major.
Brigade Major Dehra Dun Brigade...

Machine Gun Operation Orders

LA GORGUE 17th Sept

Reference sheets 36 & 36 a.

1. The Machine Guns Dehra Dun Bde will relieve M G's of BAREILLY and GARHWAL Brigades on 18th Sept. All reliefs to be completed by 1 p.m.

2. There will be 9 guns in the front line and will be distributed as follows

No 1 Emplacement 2nd Gurkhas (between SIGN POST Lane and SUNKEN ST

LAFONE POST Emplacement 2nd Gurkhas

2 3 4 5 Emplacements 4 guns 4th Seaforths (from SUNKEN STREET inclusive to SOUTH MOATED GRANGE STREET inclusive)

COLVIN POST 1 gun 1st Seaforth High^rs

8. 10. 11. 12 Emplacements 9th Gurkhas

3. Three (3) guns 1st Seaforths and their teams to be located in B line with their unit

Two guns (2) 2nd Gurkhas and their teams to be located in B line with their unit

Two (2) guns (Vickers) 9th Gurkhas to stay with limbers

4. Guides for Nos 1·2·3·4·5 ~~and~~ LAFONE and COLVIN POSTS will meet gun teams at PONT DU HEM at 9 a.m and for remainder at 9.30 a.m

5. All spare men not required in trenches to remain with M.G section limbers and will be located in a house on LA BASSEE road at present occupied by 1st line 58th Rifles.

6. All teams will proceed to trenches via ~~Rug~~ ROGBY ROAD and must take every precaution

7. Ten 10 belt boxes to be carried up to front line trench remainder to be left with M G. O 1st Seaforths and M. G. O 2nd Gurkhas in B line.

Any team unable to carry up all their ammunition can leave it at ROGBY ROAD in charge of a sentry and it can be sent for later.

8. Reports to me at M 8 d

Issued at 4 p.m.

Forwarded to O.C. units for information

J. L. Chichester Lamb Capt

Brigade Machine Gun Officer

Dehra Dun Brigade

MOVEMENT TABLE 18 – 9 – 15

Unit	To relieve.	Location.	Time of arrival at Junction of communicating Trench and RUE BACQUEROT.	ROUTE	REMARKS
4th Seaforths.	3rd Londons Garhwal Rifles.	IND. 5. A (SUNKEN ROAD exclusive but including DUCKS BILL, to SOUTH MOATED GRANGE STREET inclusive).	7 - 15 p.m.	Road junction G.32.a.2/1 - LA BASSEE road - RUE BACQUEROT - SOUTH TILLELOY STREET.	C.Os will be at new H.Q at 10 am on 17th Instant.
1 Coy 2nd Gurkhas	3rd Londons	IND. 5. A. - SIGN POST LANE exclusive to SUNKEN ROAD (DUCKS BILL exclusive).	7-15 pm.	ESTAIRES - LA BASSEE Road - RUE BACQUEROT - SUNKEN STREET.	" " " " "
9th Gurkhas.	33rd Punjabis. 2 Coys 4th Black Watch. 1 Coy 69th Punjabis. 1 Coy 2nd Black Watch.	IND. 5. B. - SOUTH MOATED GRANGE STREET exclusive to WINCHESTER ROAD inclusive	7. pm.	ESTAIRES - LA BASSEE ROAD. - RUGBY ROAD - NORTH TILLELOY and BIRD CAGE STREETS.	" " " " "
2nd Gurkhas (less 1 Coy).	2/8th Gurkhas.	B. lines South of MOATED GRANGE STREET.	7 - 30 pm.	ESTAIRES - LA BASSEE ROAD - RUE BACQUEROT - SUNKEN STREET.	" " " " "
1st Seaforths.	58th Rifles.	B lines North of MOATED GRANGE STREET.	7 - 30 pm	Road junction G.32.a.2/1 - LA BASSEE road - RUGBY ROAD - NORTH TILLELOY and BIRD CAGE STREETS.	" " " " "
Grenadier Company.		Billets M.8.d.	6 pm at M.8.d.	Road junction G.32.a.2/1. - LA. BASSEE ROAD.	
machine Guns.	Relief to be completed by 1. pm. on 18th September under arrangements of			Bde machine Gun officer.	
Bomb guns.	Relief to be completed by 1. pm on 18th September under arrangements			of Bde Bomb Gun officer	
40 men 2nd Gurkhas 1. M. Gun.	4th Cavalry.	LAFONE POST.	10 - 45 am.	ESTAIRES - LA BASSEE ROAD - RUE BACQUEROT - SUNKEN STREET.	
40 men 1st Seaforths 1. M. Gun.	4th Cavalry.	COLVIN POST	11 am.	Road junction G.32.a.2/1. - LA BASSEE ROAD - RUE BACQUEROT - S. TILLELOY STREET & COLVIN STREET	
40 men 1st Seaforths.	58th Rifles	NORTH TILLELOY POST.	11 - 15 am	Road junction G.32.a.2/1 - LA BASSEE road - RUGBY ROAD - MIN STREET	
30 men 2nd Gurkhas.	2/8th Gurkhas	SOUTH TILLELOY POST.	11-30 am.	ESTAIRES - LA BASSEE Road - RUGBY ROAD - SOUTH TILLELOY STREET	

SECRET

Head Quarters Dehra Dun Brigade.

29th September 1915.

Copy of a letter from Indian Corps to Meerut Division. No 188.I.M. dated the 12th September 1915. received under Meerut Division_s No I.G.216, dated 29th September 1915.

. ...

In the event of our coming into possession of towns or villages held by the enemy, it would be advisable to subject to a vigorous examination all persons found in, or known to be connected with, houses marked by the enemy "Gute Leute, Zu schonon" or "zu schonon: alles vergeben".

They should on no account be allowed to leave the town or village unless found to be satisfactory.

The cellars of houses should be carefully examined for underground telephone communications.

Requisition slips given by the Germans should be collected and sent to the General Staff for identification purposes.

No B.M.14.

To.

All Units.

For information and guidance.

Major.
Brigade Major Dehra Dun Brigade.

SECRET

Head Quarters Dehra Dun Brigade.

O.B. No B.5298. 20th September 1915.

1st Army.

The following instructions are issued in order to conform with similar instructions issued to the French Army in order to oviate the danger of firing upon Friendly airships.

2. No fire will be directed against an airship except by the order of an Officer.

3. At night, French Dirigibles will be supplied with a signal which they will "make" at their discretion.

4. This signal will be made by a rocket fired vertically downwards, and releasing in succession three spray showers of lights. These showers will each be the same colour. This colour will be changed from time to time, due notice being given by the French Aeronautical authorities.

5. All Officers will be notified in confidence of the nature of the signal, and of the current decision as to the colour of the showers, all precautions being taken to keep the information from becoming public property.

6. From March 24th until Noon on 20th September the colour of the showers will be "WHITE", after that date the colour will be "GREEN".

No B.M.6.

To.

The Officer Commanding

1st Seaforth Highlanders.
4th Seaforth Highlanders.
9th Gurkha Rifles.
2nd Gurkha Rifles.

Forwarded for information and guidance .

Cu Thornhill Capt for

Major.

Brigade Major Dehra Dun Brigade.

B.M.25

SECRET

INSTRUCTIONS FOR RELIEF OF IND. 5. A. by GARHWAL BRIGADE.

:-:-:-:-:-:-:-:-:-:-:-:

1. The following reliefs will be carried out by day:-

TRENCH MORTARS.
BOMB GUNS.
BRIGADE MACHINE GUNS.

2. When the arrival of relieving troops is expected all Dehra Dun Brigade troops will vacate ~~old and~~ New Support lines and collect in ~~Fire trenches~~ OLD SUPPORT TRENCH (Amd B.M.17.). The Inspection Trench is to be kept clear.

Men for whom there is no room may be sent back at once via Inspection Trench and LAFONE STREET .

3. 2/8th Gurkhas will enter via COLVIN STREET. Head of Column will halt while al DEHRA DUN BRIGADE Troops North of COLVIN STREET file away via Inspection Trench and LAFONE STREET.

4. 2nd Leicesters will occupy a part of trench South of COLVIN STREET. Their flank is marked by a signboard. They will follow 2/8th Gurkhas, when an Officer GARHWAL BRIGADE ~~are~~ announces 2nd Leicesters are approaching DEHRA DUN BRIGADE troops occupying 2nd Leicester Front South of COLVIN STREET will file away via Inspection Trench and LAFONE STREET.

5. 2/3rd Gurkhas will enter via SOUTH TILLELOY STREET. Head of Column will halt while all DEHRA DUN BRIGADE Troops North of SOUTH TILLELOY STREET file away via Inspection trench and LAFONE STREET.

6. 2/3rd Gurkhas will occupy a part of trench South of SOUTH TILLELOY STREET. Their flank is marked by a signboard. DEHRA DUN BRIGADE Troops occupying 2/3rd Gurkha front South of SOUTH TILLELOY STREET will file away via Inspection trench and LAFONE STREET as soon as an Officer GARHWAL BRIGADE reports relief approaching.

7. 3rd Londons enter by SUNKEN STREET. DEHRA DUN BRIGADE Troops relieved by 3rd Londons will file away via LAFONE STREET as relieved.

8. An Officer will be posted where Support line meets COLVIN, SOUTH TILLELOY and SUNKEN STREETS to:-

to:-

(1). Give notice of approach of relieving Units.

(2). Pass orders of GARHWAL BRIGADE Officer similarly employed.

Please acknowledge receipt

[illegible] Major

Bde. Major [illegible] Bde.

20-9-15

[illegible]

Copy of a memorandum No.S.704 dated 20th September 1915, from D.D.S.T., 1st Army, to Indian Corps, received under Indian Corps.No.3/37/S.T. dated 21st September 1915.

. . . .

At your request I have ordered two loadings of Rum to arrive at Railhead, one on the 23rd and one 24th instant. One will be for immediate issue to each Division, the other should be retained as a reserve at Railhead, to be drawn when required by the Corps.

A double ration of cheese has been ordered also, to arrive at Railhead on the 23rd instant for immediate issue to each Division as an extra havresack ration - to each Division that has not already drawn an extra ration.

Memorandum.

Forwarded for information. The rum and cheese ration will be issued at Refilling Point on the 24th instant.

Captain.
D.A.A. & Q.M.G., Meerut Division.

No.Q.10/25. 22nd September 1915.

Dehra Dun Bde.	7	C.R.A.	20	Salvage Coy.	1
Garhwal "	7	C.R.E.	6	Camp Comdt.	1
Bareilly "	7	A.D.M.S.	8	O.C.Train	6
107th Pioneers.	1	A.D.V.S.	1	S.S.O.	2
4th Cavalry.	1	Signal Coy.	1		

W.H.B.

4th Seaforths

Secret   B.M. 6   21.9.15

Instructions for Battalions of DEHRA DUN Brigade on the day of assault.

1- As the assaulting troops go forward & vacate their assembly positions the Brigade will move forward & concentrate as shown on attached table.

2- 1st Seaforths will maintain touch with 58th Rifles & 2nd Gurkhas will maintain touch with 39th Garhwalis & will keep G.O.C informed as these troops leave their assembly places.

3- In the event of all troops of both advanced brigades moving forward from our fire trench, piquets of 1 N.C.O. & 9 men will be posted every 100 yards in the fire trench. 2nd Gurkhas will find these piquets in IND. 5 A & 1st Seaforths in IND. 5 B. In the event of further advance these piquets will rejoin their units.

[illegible] Major

Bd. Major Dehra Dun Brigade

Operation order 55
by
Brigadier General W. J. St J. HARVEY
Commanding Dehra Dun Bde

Secret 4

22nd. September 1915

REFERENCE TRENCH MAP[2]
MAP OF FRANCE 1/40000

1. Information

The 1st Army is resuming the offensive in the Southern part of the line. The Indian and other Corps not engaged in the Main Offensive are carrying out local operations all along the 1st Army front.

The Indian Corps will:–

(a) attack the enemy's line between SUNKEN ROAD and WINCHESTER ROAD and establish our line along the road running through MAUQUISSART to the DUCKS BILL.

(b) Press on with its left in front, till its left gains the high ground between HAUT POMMEREAU and LA CLIQUETERIE FERME.

(c) Continue its advance from there in a South Easterly direction.

The Meerut Division will make the attack to be delivered by the Indian Corps. Lahore and 20th Divisions will co-operate in the attack and advance and maintain touch when the Meerut Division advances beyond the enemy's first and Second line trenches.

2. Intention.

The Garhwal and Bareilly Brigades will make the assault.

The Dehra Dun Brigade will be in Divisional Reserve.

3. Trench Mortar Batteries

After the assault No 5 Trench Mortar Battery will be attached to the Brigade.

4. Machine Guns.

Two Machine Guns will remain with each Battalion at disposition of Battalion Commander.

Remaining machine guns will be Brigaded under orders of Brigade Machine Gun Officer

5 Fire on Enemy's Trenches. During the deliberate bombardment the Brigade will maintain rifle, rifle grenade and Machine Gun fire by day and night in accordance with instructions already issued.

6 Positions of Assembly. The boundary line between Garhwal and Bareilly Brigades will run from M.30.c.0/4 parallel to COLVIN STREET till it cuts MOATED GRANGE STREET thence parallel to SOUTH TILLELOY STREET to "B" LINE.

On relief Dehra Dun Brigade will occupy positions of assembly as follows:—

1st Seaforths – B.LINE North of ~~MOATED GRANGE~~ SOUTH TILLELOY STREET ST.

2nd Gurkhas – B.LINE South of SOUTH TILLELOY ST.

4th Seaforths – ROUGE CROIX EAST POST and G.H.Q line North east of it.

9th Gurkhas – MIN and RUGBY POSTS and BACQUEROT STREET.

Grenadier Coy – BACQUEROT STREET.

Bde Machine Guns – BACQUEROT STREET.

7 Advanced Depots of SAA + grenades. The following advanced Depots of S.A.A and hand grenades have been formed:—

LAFONE POST } 100 boxes S.A.A and
COLVIN POST } 500 hand grenades in each.

In rear of BIRD CAGE – 1000 hand grenades

near BIRD CAGE – 100 boxes S.A.A.

Junction LAFONE STREET and RUE TILLELOY } 250 boxes S.A.A 300 rounds VERY pistol ammunition.

M.29.c.0/6 where Tram line crosses RUE TILLELOY } 1000 Hand grenades

The trench ammunition of "B" LINE has been assembled by the assaulting Bdes in Depots in the front line. The above Depots have been marked by notice boards and direction arrows have been ~~have been~~ erected in the front line to point out the way to the nearest ammunition

ammunition or hand grenade Depot.
The positions of these Depots are to be explained to all ranks.

8.
R.E. Stores. Advanced Depots of R.E. Stores have been formed at:-
DUCKS BILL.
NECK of DUCKS BILL
M.30.c.0/4.
HEAD of COLVIN STREET.
In rear of the BIRD CAGE.

9
Medical. Collecting Stations are ~~collected~~ established in Dug outs as follows:-
(i). M.28.d.8/4 near the junction of LAFONE STREET and RUE TILLELOY.
(ii) M.28.d.6/2.
(iii) M.34.b.5/9. EBENEZER FARM.
Wounded will reach the collecting Stations by LAFONE STREET or by NORTH or SOUTH MOATED GRANGE STREETS and MOATED GRANGE STREET or by TRAM STREET and TILLELOY TRENCH TRAM LINE.
Advanced Dressing Station is at M.14.c.3/1, and the route from Collecting Stations is by the tram lines or by EBENEZER STREET to M.21.d.7/1 and thence by the tram line. Only the above communication trenches are specially adopted to take stretchers.

10
Traffic Traffic in the long communication trenches must move in accordance with the direction arrows. The following have been marked for traffic moving from our rear to our front:-
SUNKEN STREET – COLVIN STREET.
SOUTH TILLELOY STREET
NORTH TILLELOY STREET
BIRD CAGE STREET

The following have been marked for traffic moving from our front to our rear:–

EBENEZER STREET.
MOATED GRANGE STREET
MIN STREET
LAFONE STREET
SOUTH MOATED GRANGE STREET
NORTH MOATED GRANGE STREET
TRAM STREET.

These traffic rules may be broken for urgent tactical reasons only.

11
Trench Police. Traffic control posts will be posted by the Staff Captain at 5 pm on the day preceding assault as follows:–

Junction MOATED GRANGE STREET and SOUTH TILLELOY STREET.
Junction MOATED GRANGE STREET and SUNKEN STREET.
Junction MIN STREET and RUE DU BACQUEROT.
Junction EBENEZER STREET & RUE DU BACQUEROT.

Each post will consist of one British and one Indian Soldier.

12.
Distinguishing flags. The following distinguishing flags will be carried to assist in showing the localities reached by our troops:– Garhwal Bde BLUE with RED bar
Bareilly Bde BLACK with YELLOW bar
Dehra Dun Bde plain YELLOW.

The flags are 2' square and bars are 8" broad.

Distinguishing flags of Divisions on right and left are:–

LAHORE DIV – YELLOW with black stripe in centre – Flag 2'-6" square.

20th DIV – Top half GREEN bottom half PINK Flag 2" square.

A Coloured diagram of these flags has been issued.

13. Daylight Rockets — Daylight rockets to inform the Artillery that the Infantry is making a further advance will be carried. These rockets will be used in bunches of several fired simultaneously. This signal should be used only if the ordinary communications are interupted. After the assault has been launched no other signal will be made by daylight. Rockets of Garhwal Brigade are RED. Those of Bareilly and Dehra Dun Bdes are BLUE.

14. Prisoners. — Prisoners will be sent to Brigade Head Quarters under escort. They are to be searched for documents and other articles as soon as possible after being captured. These must accompany the prisoners and be handed over from one escort to another.

15. Sandbags. — Each man will carry two sandbags.

16. Packs — Packs will not be carried. Arrangements will be made to stack packs during the night preceding assault or on morning of assault as follows:—

1st Seaforths — Close to WINCHESTER ROAD
2nd Gurkhas — Close to RUE TILLELOY
4th Seaforths — Close to RUE BACQUEROT
9th Gurkhas — Close to RUE BACQUEROT.

17. Transport. — From 6 pm on 24th Instant all baggage wagons and 1st line transport will be kept loaded up.

18. Entrenching tools. — 20 shovels per company will be carried. Remaining entrenching tools will be loaded on tool limbers on the night 23rd/24th under Battalion arrangements.

19 Secret documents — Secret documents, plans, sketches shewing our line will not be taken beyond present battalion Head Quarters.

20 General Instructions — The importance of advancing at all costs must be impressed on all ranks. If one portion of the line is held up there is no necessity for other portions to check.

It is most important that communication is kept up.

21 Reports. — Report Centre is at M.22.C.4/5.

Issued at ..4.p.m..

[signature] Major

Bde Major Dehra Dun Brigade

To Signal Section for distribution

Copy 1 and 2 retained
Copy 3 to 1st Seaforths
Copy 4 to 4th Seaforths
Copy 5 to 9th Gurkhas
Copy 6 to 2nd Gurkhas
Copy 7 to 93rd B. Infy
Copy 8 to Meerut Div
Copy 9 to Bareilly Bde
Copy 10 to Garhwal Bde
Copy 11 to 2 Coy Train
Copy 12 to 4th Bde RFA
Copy 13 to 13th Bde RFA.
Copy 14 to 5th Trench Battery
Copy 15 to Bde M.G.O
Copy 16 to Bde G.O
Copy 17 to Bde S.O.
Copy 18 to Bde B.G.O

SECRET

20th Div

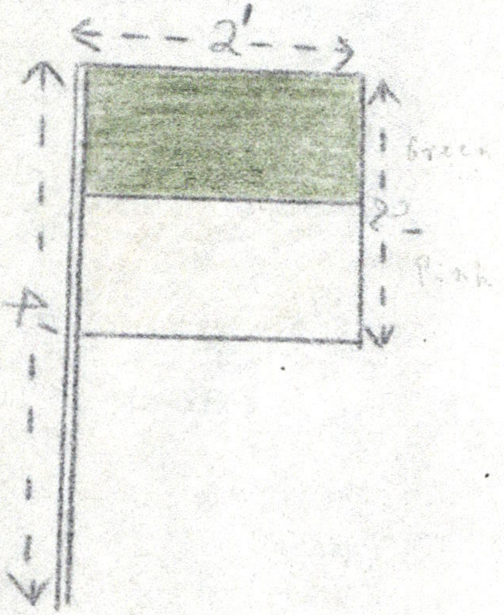

2'
2'
Green
Pink
4'

Bareilly Bde.

2'
2'
8"
Black
Yellow
Black
5'

Garhwal Bde

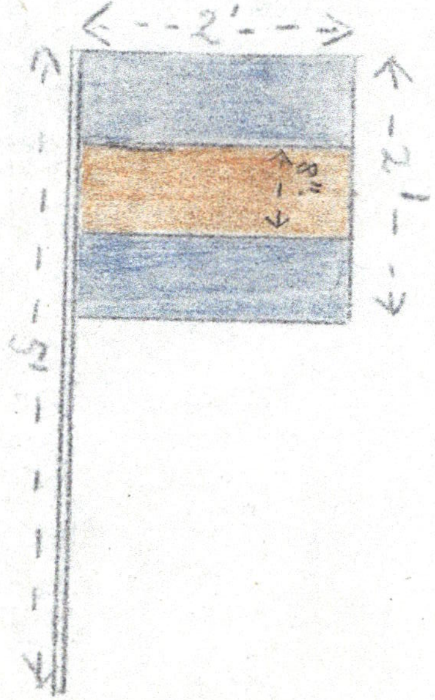

2'
2'
8"
5'

Lahore Divn

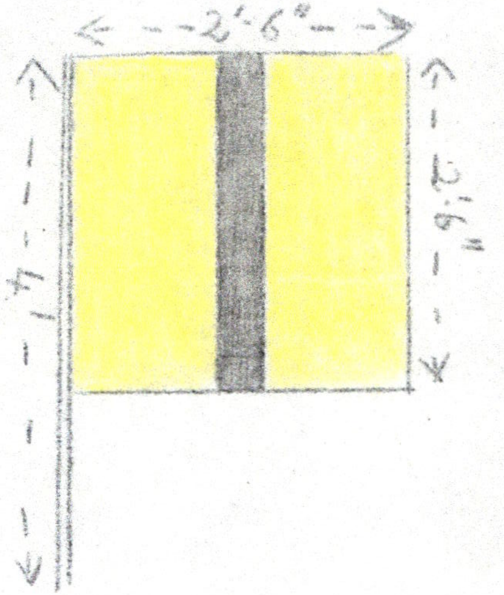

2'6"
2'6"
4'

Dehra Dun Bde

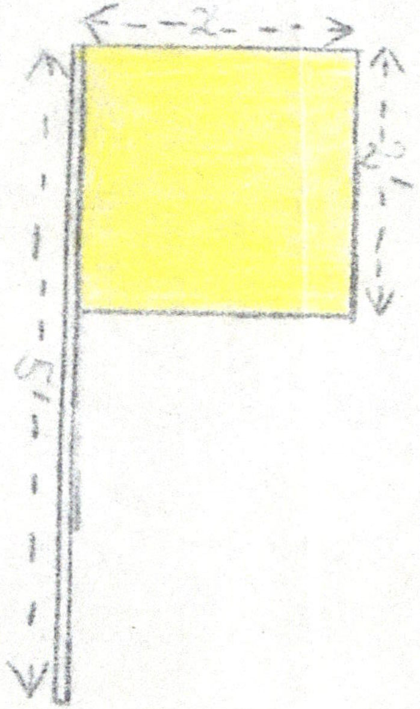

2
2'
5'

Bm 18
19-9-15

Copy No 4

OPERATION ORDER No 56

By

Brigadier General W. J. St. J. HARVEY.
Commanding Dehra Dun Brigade.

22nd September 1915.

1. During the night 23rd/24th September the line now held by the DEHRA DUN BRIGADE will be adjusted as follows:-

JULLUNDER BRIGADE will extend its front to SUNKEN ROAD exclusive. DEHRA DUN BRIGADE will extend its front to WINCHESTER STREET exclusive.

Dividing line between Subsections will be M.30.c.0/4.

2. JULLUNDER BRIGADE will relieve Company 2nd Gurkhas between SIGN POST LANE and SUNKEN ROAD. Relieved Company will rejoin Battalion in "B" LINE.

4th Seaforths will extend left to M.30.c.0/4.

9th Gurkhas will extend left to take over from 60th Brigade, front and support line trenches up to WINCHESTER STREET.

Details of reliefs will be arranged between Commanding Officers concerned.

3. Subsection Commander IND.5.B. may draw a Company 1st Seaforths in support to strengthen his line if necessary.

Issued at 4.40 p.m.

[signature] Major
Brigade Major Dehra Dun Brigade.

Issued to Signal Section for distribution.

Copy 1 and 2 retained.
Copy 3. 1st Seaforths.
Copy 4 4th Seaforths.
Copy 5 9th Gurkhas
Copy 6 2nd Gurkhas .
Copy 7. Meerut Division
Copy 8 Bareilly Bde.
Copy 9 to Garhwal Brigade.
Copy 10 to 4th Brigade R.F.A.
Copy 11 to 13th Brigade R.F.A.
Copy 12 to 2 Coy Train.
Copy 13 to Bde Machine Gun Officer
Copy 14 to Brigade Grenadier Officer
Copy 15 to Brigade Signalling Officer
Copy 16. to Brigade Bomb Gun Officer
Copy 17 to 60th Bde

SECRET.

No. G.B.486.
Meerut Division,
22nd September 1915.

The arrangements which have been made with regard to gas and smoke-candle detachments are as follows:-

Gas and smoke candle detachments will occupy their positions in each bay of the fire trench prior to the relief of Dehra Dun Brigade by Garhwal and Bareilly Bdes.

The number of men in each bay varies from two to six.

The necessity for not interfering with these men in the performance of their important duties, which commence 10 minutes before and end at the moment of assault, is impressed on all.

During the time that units of the Bareilly and Garhwal Bdes are waiting in the assembly positions, every precaution is to be taken to ensure that sentries only enter the actual bays in which the gas and smoke-candlemen are placed, and that the appliances and stores are not interfered with in any way. Infantry have, however, to come into the bays at two minutes before the assault is to be delivered, to enable them to cross the parapet and form up.

Smoke candle parties are organised into two sections, that on the right being found by the 4th Seaforths under the command of Lieut. MORRISON, 4th Seaforths, and that on the left by the 1st Seaforths under Lieut. MACNAUGHTON, 1st Seaforths.

The O.C. Left Section Smoke Det. will be near the head of MIN STREET; nearest telephone - H.Q. 2nd B.Watch, near junction of TRAM STREET and new support line, or H.Q. 33rd Punjabis, near junction of NORTH MOATED GRANGE STREET and new support line.

The O.C. Right Section, Smoke Det. will be near head of SUNKEN STREET; nearest telephones H.Q. 3rd Londons at junction of SUNKEN STREET and new support line.

The Officers i/c Gas Dets. will be located as follows:-

Lieut. KENT, O.C., at Bareilly Bde Report Centre near junction of COLVIN STREET & HOME COUNTIES TRENCH.

Lieut. TAYLOR, in charge of Gas Det in DUCKSBILL; nearest telephone, 3rd Londons in neck of DUCKSBILL.

Lieut. PICKARD, in charge of Gas Det. on salient at end of COMMIN STREET; nearest telephone - H.Q. 2nd. Leicesters at junction of COLVIN St and new support line.

Lieut. CAMPBELL SMITH, in charge of Gas Det. at salients just north of end of SOUTH MOATED GRANGE STREET and at end of NORTH TILLELOY STREET; nearest telephones- H.Q. 2/8th Gurkha Rifles and H.Q. 4th B.Watch both near junction of SOUTH MOATED GRANGE STREET and new support line.

All units and formations will please give these officers every facility in either sending or receiving messages.

P. Davies
Lieut.-Colonel,
General Staff,
Meerut Division.

To,
Dehra Dun Bde 5 copies-1 per Bn less 93rd I.
Garhwal Bde 6 ,, 1 per Bn
Bareilly Bde 6 ,, ,,
Lieut KENT 5 ,, for self & sub.-commdrs
Lieut. MORRISON, 4th Seaforths
,, MACNAUGHTON 1st Seaforths
Meerut Signals - for information of O.C. only, at present.

"A" Form. Army Form C. 2121

MESSAGES AND SIGNALS.

No. of Message

Prefix ... Code ... m.	Words	Charge	This message is on a/c of:	Recd. at ... m.
Office of Origin and Service Instructions.	Sent		... Service.	Date
Secret	At ... m.			From
Urgent	To			By
	By		(Signature of "Franking Officer.")	

TO: 1st Seaforths | 4th Seaforths | 9th Gurkhas | 2nd Gurkhas

Sender's Number.	Day of Month	In reply to Number	AAA
* B.M. 16	22		

1- All VERMOREL sprayers are to be kept filled and ready for instant use from 6 p.m. to-night.

2- All B.O.s are to be warned that as soon as the cylinders arrive in the trenches which will probably be this evening they are to warn all men that the word "gas" must not be mentioned if anyone is in the trenches. This is necessary to prevent any possibility of a German patrol overhearing it.

3- The word "gas" or "cylinders" is not to be telephoned or telegraphed under any circumstances.

4- The importance of the strictest secrecy must be impressed on all ranks.

From

Place

Time

The above may be forwarded as now corrected. (Z)

Censor. Signature of Addressor or person authorised to telegraph in his name.

* This line should be erased if not required.

(632) —McC. & Co. Ltd., London.— W 11400/2045. 100,000. 2/15. Forms C 2121/10.

AND

...ice Instructions.

Charge

Sent

At .... m.

To ....

By ....

This message is on a/c of:

.... *Service.*

(Signature of "Franking Officer.")

Recd. at .... m.

Date ....

From ....

By ....

TO

Sender's Number.	Day of Month	In reply to Number	AAA
*			

5 - Please inform all troops in your situation.

6 - Acknowledge

From	D	D	Bde
Place			
Time			

The above may be forwarded as now corrected.

.... *Censor.*

(Z) [illegible] Major B.M.

Signature of Addressor or person authorised to telegraph in his name.

* This line should be erased if not required.

(632) —McC. & Co. Ltd., London.— W 11400/2045. 100,000. 2/15. Forms C 2121/10.

"A" Form. Army Form C. 2121.

MESSAGES AND SIGNALS.

No. of Message ______

Prefix ______ Code ______ m.	Words	Charge	This message is on a/c of:	Recd. at ______ m.
Office of Origin and Service Instructions	Sent		______ Service.	Date ______
	At ______ m.			From ______
	To ______			
	By ______		(Signature of "Franking Officer.")	By ______

TO [illegible]

Sender's Number	Day of Month	In reply to Number	AAA
* [illegible]	[illegible]		

[illegible]	[illegible]	[illegible]	Medical	[illegible]
[illegible]	[illegible]	[illegible]	[illegible]	[illegible]
[illegible]	[illegible]	[illegible]	WINCHESTER	ROAD
[illegible]	[illegible]	[illegible]	[illegible]	2 a.m.
23rd [illegible]	AAA	[illegible]	[illegible]	[illegible]
[illegible]	[illegible]	[illegible]	[illegible]	[illegible]
[illegible]	[illegible]	[illegible]	[illegible]	[illegible]
[illegible]	AAA	[illegible]	[illegible]	[illegible]

From	[illegible]	[illegible]	[illegible]	
Place				
Time				

The above may be forwarded as now corrected.

(Z) [illegible]

Censor. Signature of Addressor or person authorised to telegraph in his name.

* This line should be erased if not required.

(15191) S. & Co. Ltd. W 14142/611. 90,000. 4/15. Forms C 2121/10.

C O N F I D E N T I A L

Head Quarters Dehra Dun Brigade .

22nd September 1915.

Copy of a memo from 1st Army to Indian Corps No R.A. 100/143, dated the 19th September 1915. Received under Meerut Division's No G.427, dated the 20th Sept 15.

....

Please note that the Stokes Mortar Batteries will in future be distinguished from other Trench Batteries by initial letter in alphabetical order, the word "STOKES" being dropped.

The Batteries hitherto sent to you now become:-

No 12 becomes L. Trench Mortar Battery.
No 13 becomes M. Trench Moratr Battery.

Postal Authorities have been warned.

No B.M.4.

From.

The Brigade Major

Dehra Dun Brigade.

To.

The Officer Commanding

1st Seaforths.
4th Seaforths.
9th Gurkhas.
2nd Gurkhas.

Forwarded for information.

Above Batteries have been posted as under:-

L. Trench Mortar Battery to Lahore Division.
M. Trench Mortar Battery to Meerut Division.

Major.

Brigade Major Dehra Dun Brigade.

SECRET

Head Quarters Dehra Dun Brigade.

No B.M.30. 22nd September 1915.

From.

The Brigade Major.

Dehra Dun Brigade.

In confirmation of my No's B.M.24, 26 and 29 sent by wire.

The following routes will be closed to all ordinary traffic:-from 2.a.m. to 6.a.m. on 23rd Inst for special carrying parties :-

A. SOUTH TILLELOY STREET from RUE BACQUEROT to junction with COLVIN STREET thence via COLVIN STREET to front line.
This route will be policed by Picquet No 3 - 2 Officers, 4th Seaforths, 1 Gurkha Officer and 1 N.C.O. 2nd Gurkhas.

B. NORTH TILLELOY STREET as far as RUE TILLELOY TRENCH - RUE TILLELOY TRENCH to MOATED GRANGE STREET - MOATED GRANGE STREET from RUE TILLELOY to junction NORTH and SOUTH MOATED GRANGE STREET - thence SOUTH MOATED GRANGE STREET.
This route will be policed by Picquet No 2 2 British Officers 2nd Gurkhas - 2 N.C.O's 2nd Gurkhas.

C MIN STREET as far as RUE TILLELOY TRENCH - RUE TILLELOY TRENCH from MIN STREET to NORTH TILLELOY STREET - NORTH TILLELOY STREET from RUE TILLELOY TRENCH to FRONT LINE.
This route will be policed by Picquet No 1 2 Officers 1st Seaforths 1 Gurkha Officer 1 N.C.O. 2nd Gurkhas.

Carrying Parties will come up these routes and return by same routes.

Major
Brigade Major Dehra Dun Bde.

UNIT.	PLACE.	HEAD QUARTERS.	ROUTE.
2nd Gurkhas.	HOME COUNTIES TRENCH, SOUTH of COLVIN STREET.	Near COLVIN STREET.	SUNKEN STREET and SOUTH TILLOLEY STREET
1st Seaforths	Trench along N Edge of RUE TILLELOY.	Near Junction MIN STREET and RUE TILLELOY.	NORTH TILLELOY and BIRDCAGE STREETS.
4th Seaforths	"B" LINE, South of SOUTH TILLELOY STREET	Junction LAFONE STREET and "B" LINE.	SUNKEN STREET.
9th Gurkhas	"B" LINE, North of MOATED GRANGE STREET.	Junction NORTH TILLELOY STREET and "B" LINE.	1 Coy via SOUTH TILLELOY STREET (To follow Bde Machine Guns) 2 Coys via NORTH TILLELOY STREET. 1 Coy via BIRD CAGE STREET
Grenadier Company.	HOME COUNTIES TRENCH, NORTH OF COLVIN STREET.	Junction COLVIN & HOME COUNTIES TRENCH.	SOUTH TILLELOY STREET.
Bde Machine Guns.	HOME COUNTIES Trench North of COLVIN STREET.	Junction COLVIN & HOME COUNTIES TRENCH.	SOUTH TILLELOY STREET (To follow Grenadier Company).
Bde Head Quarters.	BAREILLY BRIGADE Advanced Report Centre.	Junction COLVIN STREET and HOME COUNTIES TRENCH.	SOUTH TILLELOY STREET

Secret

The O.C.
Ind. S–B
11. 5–15

I made a most careful inspection of the firing line steps running and found that certain of the sand bag steps had been removed. Will you please issue orders that these are remade today. It is of the utmost importance that the steps are in perfect order when this Brigade leaves the firing line.

23.9.15 J H T Hardy Brig Genl
Dehra Dun Bde

28

Secret

Head Quarters Dehra Dun Brigade.

No B.M. 11.

23rd September 1915.

From.

The Brigade Major.

Dehra Dun Brigade.

To.

The Officer Commanding
1st Seaforths.
4th Seaforths.
9th Gurkhas.
2nd Gurkhas.

1. Carrying Parties as under will be found tonight. They will be at Farm at M.32.b.8/8 at North end of BACQUEROT STREET at 1-30.a.m. on 24th Instant. Parties will be met by three Officers of special Company.

<u>No 1 party</u> 2nd Gurkhas.- 2 British Officers, 1 Gurkha Officer, 4 N.C.O's and 72 Carriers.

Route:- From BACQUEROT STREET up SUNKEN STREET thence up LAFONE STREET as far as LAFONE POST thence to SUNKEN ROAD and DUCKS BILL.

<u>No 2 Party</u> 2nd Gurkhas - 2 British officers, 1 Gurkha Officer, 2.N.C.O's and 33 Carriers.

Route:- From BACQUEROT STREET up BIRDCAGE STREET turn left on RUE TILLELOY up TRAM STREET along FRONT LINE to end of WINCHESTER STREET.

<u>No 3 Party.</u> 9th Gurkhas:- 2 British Officers, 1 Gurkha Officer, 3 N.C.O's and 54 Carriers.

Route- from BACQUEROT STREET up ~~XXX~~ BIRDCAGE STREET turn left on RUE TILLELOY up TRAM STREET to front line.

2. Parties will return by same routes and deposit [illegible] at Farm M.32.b.8/8 afterwards rejoining their Units.

3. No Arms or equipment except gas helmets will be carried.

4. The routes to be followed will be closed from 1 to 6.a.m. Traffic control parties for each route will be found as under:-

Route of Party No 1 - 2 Officers and 2 N.C.O's - 1st Seaforths.

Route of parties No 2 and 3 - 2 Officers and 3 N.C.O's 1st Seaforths.

5. Medical Officer 2nd Gurkhas will accompany Party No 1. Medical Officer 9th Gurkhas will accompany Parties No 2 & 3.

Major.
Brigade Major Dehra Dun Brigade.

No. B.M. 27.

Head Quarters Dehra Dun Brigade.

SECRET

23rd September 1915.

From.

The Brigade Major.

Dehra Dun Brigade.

With a view to reducing Casualties among Officers and in order to have a Reserve immediately available to replace casualties as they occur only such Officers as are absolutely required will accompany their Units into action and in no case will the number with a British Infantry Battalion exceed 20 including Battalion Head Quarters and in an ~~Infantry~~ Indian Battalion at full strength not more than 11 Officers including Battalion Head Quarters will be taken into action. Regiments under full strength in proportion.

Major.

Brigade Major Dehra Dun Brigade.

To.

The Officer Commanding

1st Seaforths
4th Seaforths.
9th Gurkhas.
2nd Gurkhas.

"A" Form. Army Form C. 2121.

MESSAGES AND SIGNALS.

No. of Message

Prefix	Code	m.	Words	Charge	This message is on a/c of:	Recd. at m.
Office of Origin and Service Instructions			Sent		Service.	Date
Sent			At m.			From
			To			
			By		(Signature of "Franking Officer.")	By

TO			
1st Seaforths	4th Seaforths	9th Gordons	2nd Gordons

* Sender's Number	Day of Month	In reply to Number	AAA
BM 20	23rd		

all	ranks	assembling	in	front
of	B	line	in	[illegible]
prior	to	assault	to	day
by	assault	will	wear	old
pattern	smoke	helmet	rolled	up
is	so	arranged	as	to
be	able	to	be	pulled
down	on	the	head	& face
at	a	moments	notice	AAA
Tube	helmets	will	also	be
carried	by	all	ranks	in
the	usual	manner		

From	D	D	Bde	
Place				
Time				

The above may be forwarded as now corrected.

Censor.

(Z) [illegible] Major B.M.

Signature of Addressor or person authorised to telegraph in his name.

* This line should be erased if not required.

(15191) S. & Co. Ltd. W 14142/611. 90,000. 4/15. Forms C 2121/10.

"A" Form. Army Form C. 21–

MESSAGES AND SIGNALS.

No. of Message

Prefix Code m.	Words 21	Charge	This message is on a/c of:	Recd. at 9.48 p m.
Office of Origin and Service Instructions	Sent		Service.	Date 23/9/15
	At m.			From RFT
	To			
	By		(Signature of "Franking Officer.")	By Humphrys

TO ADJT

Sender's Number	Day of Month	In reply to Number	AAA
* CH 4	23rd		

1406	Pte	MORE	is	with the
No	2	Coy	in	the
firing	line			

From	O	C	
Place	No 2	COY	
Time			

The above may be forwarded as now corrected. (Z)

Censor. Signature of Addressor or person authorised to telegraph in his name.

* This line should be erased if not required.

(15491) S. & Co. Ltd. W 14142/641. 90,000. 4/15. Forms C 2121/10.

interfered ~~interfe~~

SALIENT

interfered

interfered

interfered

interfered

interfered

interfered

interfered

in interfered

Geo. interfered

Sir John Ross France

~~Sir John Ross France~~ Prince

I S ~~[illegible]~~

And And as [illegible] were sitting down. But however war is war! And [illegible] And [illegible] with a tall, [illegible] white-haired chap with gold rimmed spectacles. He got [illegible]

[illegible]

"A" Form. Army Form C. 2121.

MESSAGES AND SIGNALS. No. of Message

Prefix SB Code 1RSA m.	Words 26	Charge	This message is on a/c of:	Recd. at 9.40A m.
Office of Origin and Service Instructions. 215 Priority	Sent At m. To By		Service. (Signature of "Franking Officer.")	Date 21/8 From 2 I By Law W

TO 4th Seaforths

Sender's Number	Day of Month	In reply to Number	AAA
* BM 5	23		

Bde direct LIEUT MORRISON to be at B subsection HQ at 11 am to meet COL DAVIES aaa acknowledge

From II Div Bde

Place

Time

The above may be forwarded as now corrected. (Z)

Censor. Signature of Addressor or person authorised to telegraph in his name.

* This line should be erased if not required.

202146--W. & S. Ltd., London,—W 14142/641—90,000—4/15. Forms C 2121/10.

OPERATION ORDER NO 57.

by

Brigadier General W. J. ST. J. HARVEY.

Commanding Dehra Dun Brigade.

23rd September 1915.

Secret

Reference Trench Map.

1. The GARHWAL and BAREILLY BRIGADES will relieve DEHRA DUN BRIGADE in IND.5. trenches.

2. Reliefs will be carried out in accordance with attached movement table and special instructions already issued.

3. Garrisons of NORTH and SOUTH TILLELOY POSTS will rejoin their Units in "B" LINE at 6-30.p.m. on 24th Instant.

4. From 6.p.m. on 24th Instant no troops except sentries are to be in the bays utilized for a special purpose.

5. Reports to M.22.c.4/5.

issued at. 10-15 p.m. Major

Brigade Major Dehra Dun Brigade

Copy No 1 and 2 retained.
Copy No 3 to 1st Seaforths.
Copy No 4 to 4th Seaforths.
Copy No 5 to 9th Gurkhas.
Copy No 6 to 2nd Gurkhas
Copy No 7 to 93rd Burmah Infantry
Copy No 8 to Meerut Division
Copy No 9 to Bareilly Brigade.
Copy No 10 to Garhwal Brigade.
Copy No 11 to 2 Coy Meerut Train.
Copy No 12 to 4th Brigade R.F.A.
Copy No 13 to 13th Brigade R.F.A.
Copy No 14 to 5th Trench Morter Battery
Copy No 15 to Bde Machine Gun Officer
Copy No 16 to Brigade Grenadier Officer
Copy No 17 to Brigade Bomb Gun Officer
Copy No 18 to Brigade Signalling Officer.
Copy No 19 to Jullunder Bde
Copy No 20 to 60th Brigade.

MOVEMENT TABLE.

UNIT	Location	To be relieved by.	Destination	Route	Headquarters	Remarks.
4th Seaforths	IND. 5. A	Garhwal Bde	ROUGE CROIX EAST POST on G. H. Q. line.	INSPECTION TRENCH – LAFONE STREET – EBENEZER ST.	M. 28. a. 5/8.	
9th Gurkhas	IND. 5. B.	Bareilly Brigade	RUGBY. POST. MIN POST BACQUEROT STREET.	Inspection Trench – BIRDCAGE STREET.	M. 22. c. 8/7.	
Grenadier Coy	M. 8. d and IND. 5. A.	—	BACQUEROT ST from SOUTH TILLELOY STREET to 100 yards west.	RUGBY ROAD	M. 22. c. ~~8/7~~ 4/5	To be in position by 6-30 pm
Bde Machine Guns	IND 5	Garhwal and Bareilly Machine Guns	BACQUEROT ST from Grenadier Coy to 60 yards West of SUNKEN ROAD.	M. 22. c. 4/5	M. 22. C. 4/5.	Relief by day under orders of Bde M. G. O
Bde Bomb Guns	IND. 5.		Dug outs M. 23. c. 3/9.		M. 22. c. 4/5	Relief by day under orders of Bde Bomb gun Officer
93rd Infantry	BEAUPRE FARM.		CARTERS POST M. 8. a. 9/10.	LA GORGUE – Road Junction G. 32. a. 2/1 – LA BASSEE ROAD	CARTERS POST	

N.B. ALL TIMES WILL BE NOTIFIED LATER BY WIRE OR MOTOR CYCLIST.

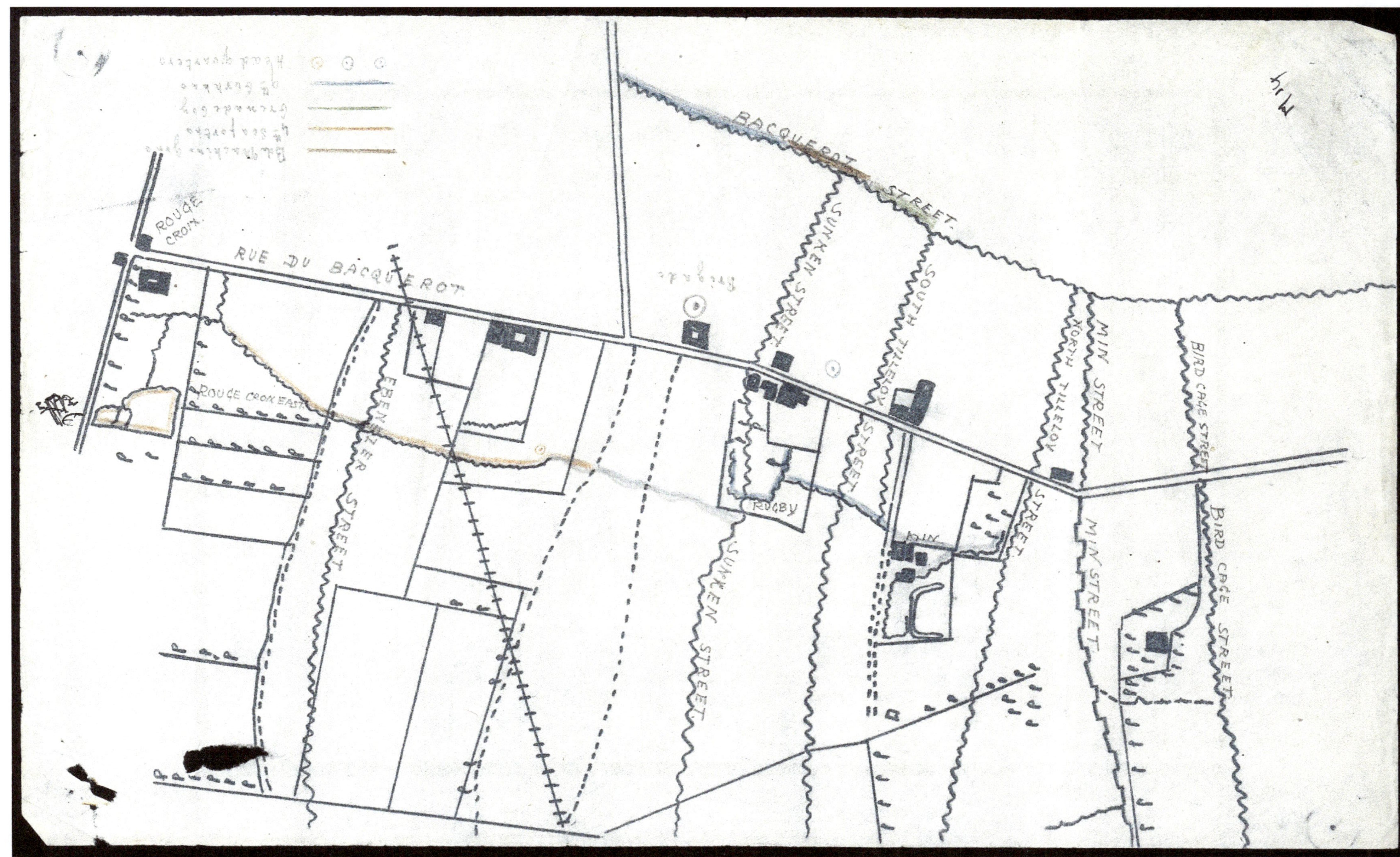

ROUGE CROIX
RUE DU BACQUEROT
ROUGE CROIX EAST
EBENEZER STREET
Brigade
SUNKEN STREET
SUNKEN STREET
RUGBY
SOUTH TILLELOY
STREET
BACQUEROT STREET
NORTH TILLELOY
STREET
MIN STREET
MIN STREET
BIRD CAGE STREET
BIRD CAGE STREET
Head quarters
M 14

"A" Form. Army Form C. 2121.

MESSAGES AND SIGNALS. No. of Message

Prefix ... Code ... m. Office of Origin and Service Instructions.	Words 46	Charge	This message is on a/c of: ... Service. (Signature of "Franking Officer.")	Recd. at P m. Date 21SR From ESKY By
	Sent At ... m. To ... By ...			

TO 4th Seaforths

Sender's Number	Day of Month	In reply to Number	AAA
*BM21	24th		

a	hole	has	been	made
by	a	shell	in	EBENEZER
STREET	aaa	please	arrange	to
repair	it	and	report	when
done	aaa	when	repairing	~~hole~~
~~not~~	~~repair~~	look	out	for
telephone	wires	aaa	the	hole
is	about	400	yards	from
RUE	BACQUEROT			

From
Place D ... D Bde
Time

The above may be forwarded as now corrected. (Z)

Censor. Signature of Addressor or person authorised to telegraph in his name.

* This line should be erased if not required.

202146—W. & S. Ltd., London.—W 14142/641—90,000—4/15. Forms C 2121/10.

"A" Form. Army Form C. 2121.

MESSAGES AND SIGNALS. No. of Message

Prefix ... Code ... m.	Words 29	Charge	This message is on a/c of:	Recd. at 2.10 P m.
Office of Origin and Service Instructions.	Sent		... Service.	Date ZS.
	At ... m.			From
	To			
	By		(Signature of "Franking Officer.")	By Esky

TO 4th Seaforths

Sender's Number	Day of Month	In reply to Number	AAA
*BM 14	24th		

headquarters		Dehra	Dun	Brigade
will	close	at	M.8D	at
2.30	pm	and	open	at
advanced	report	centre	M22C45	
at	3.	pm		

From
Place D D Bole
Time

The above may be forwarded as now corrected. (Z)

Censor. Signature of Addressor or person authorised to telegraph in his name.

* This line should be erased if not required.

20216—W. & S. Ltd., London.—W 14142/641—90,000—4/15. Forms C 2121/10.

"A" Form. Army Form C. 2121.

MESSAGES AND SIGNALS. No. of Message

Prefix ... Code ... m.	Words 13	Charge		Recd. at p. m.
Office of Origin and Service Instructions.	Sent		This message is on a/c of: ... Service.	Date 7/5
	At ... m.			From
	To			By Esky
	By		(Signature of "Franking Officer.")	

TO 4th Seaforths

*Sender's Number	Day of Month	In reply to Number	AAA
BM 11	24th	919	

impossible to reduce garrison

From
Place D D Bde
Time

The above may be forwarded as now corrected. (Z)

Censor. Signature of Addressor or person authorised to telegraph in his name.

* This line should be erased if not required.

202146--W. & S. Ltd., London.--W 14142/641--90,000--4/15. Forms C 2121/10.

"A" Form.

Army Form C. 2121.

MESSAGES AND SIGNALS.

No. of Message

Prefix ... Code ... m.	Words 22	Charge	This message is on a/c of:	Recd. at 10.17a m.
Office of Origin and Service Instructions.	Sent		Service.	Date 25
	At ... m.			From
	To			
	By		(Signature of "Franking Officer.")	By Esky

TO { 1st Seaforths 4th Seaforths
9th Gurkhas 2nd Gurkhas

Sender's Number	Day of Month	In reply to Number	
* BM8	24th		AAA

Please	do	your	best	to
~~leave~~	leave	the	line	in
as	good	order	as	possible

From
Place D D Bde
Time

The above may be forwarded as now corrected. (Z)

Censor. Signature of Addressor or person authorised to telegraph in his name.

* This line should be erased if not required.

202146--W. & S. Ltd., London.—W 14142/641—90,000—4/15. Forms C 2121/10.

"A" Form. Army Form C. 2121.

MESSAGES AND SIGNALS.

No. of Message ....

Prefix........ Code .... m. Office of Origin and Service Instructions.	Words	Charge	This message is on a/c of: .... Service. (Signature of "Franking Officer.")	Recd. at .... m. Date .... From .... By ....
	Sent At .... m. To .... By			

TO { O C No 2 Company

Sender's Number.	Day of Month	In reply to Number	AAA
*			

Brigade Grenadiers to be at Junction of Rugby Road and Rue Du Bacquerot at 6 pm where a Guide will meet them from the Brigade Company of Grenadiers

From
Place O C 4th Seaforths
Time

The above may be forwarded as now corrected.

.... *Censor.*

(Z)

Signature of Addressor or person authorised to telegraph in his name.

* This line should be erased if not required.

(688-9) —McC. & Co. Ltd., London.— W 14142/641. 225,000 4/15. Forms C 2121/10.

"A" Form.

Army Form C. 2121.

MESSAGES AND SIGNALS.

No. of Message

Prefix ... Code ... m.	Words	Charge	This message is on a/c of:	Recd. at ... m.
Office of Origin and Service Instructions	Sent At ... m. To ... By ...		... Service. (Signature of "Franking Officer.")	Date ... From ... By ...

TO				
	4th	Suffolks		
	2nd	Gurkhas		

Sender's Number	Day of Month	In reply to Number	AAA
* B.M. 17	24th		

Relieving	units	will	begin	to
arrive	on	RUE	BACQUEROT	at
9 p.m.				

From	D	D	Bde	
Place				
Time				

The above may be forwarded as now corrected.

(Z) [illegible] Major B.M.

Censor. Signature of Addressor or person authorised to telegraph in his name.

* This line should be erased if not required.

(15191) S. & Co. Ltd. W 14142/611. 90,000. 4/15. Forms C 2121/10.

S E C R E T.

NOT TO BE CARRIED FORWARD BEYOND OUR FRONT PARAPET UNDER ANY CIRCUMSTANCES.

P R O G R A M M E "A".

TIME TABLE if GAS and SMOKE are EMPLOYED.

-0.2 (i.e., 2 minutes before ZERO) Mine fired.
0.0 Daylight rocket signal sent up from Bareilly Brigade Hdqrs (near junction of COLVIN St and HOME COUNTIES TRENCH.).
0.0 Commencement of GAS.
0.0 Artillery, except guns in our parapet, open shrapnel fire on the enemy's front trenches, and H.E. fire on enemy's defences further in rear.
0.4 Two field guns and Hotchkiss gun in our front parapet open fire.
0.5 Smoke screens on flanks commence.
0.5 Smoke commences along entire front concurrently with the Gas.
0.8 Gas to be cut off.
0.8 Infantry fill up all bays of the fire trench and get into pos-ition to cross our parapet.
0.9 Infantry cross our parapet and form up.
0.9 Artillery lifts 100 yards.
0.9 Field gun in our front trench near the BIRDCAGE ceases fire.
0.10 Assault commences.
0.10 Field gun in our front trench near DUCKS BILL ceases fire.
0.11 Artillery lifts another 100 yards.
0.14 Artillery lifts to German 2nd position about 500 yards in rear of their front trench.
0.15 Smoke screens on flanks stop, but the smoke has still to disperse.
0.20 Hotchkiss gun in our front parapet ceases fire.

PROGRAMME "B"

TIME TABLE if GAS and SMOKE are N O T EMPLOYED.

4.20 A.M. By this time the assaulting infantry are to be lying in position outside our parapet.
4.25 A.M. Artillery bombardment commences including guns in our front parapet.
4.27 A.M. MINE exploded.

4.30 A.M. Assault.

4.30 A.M. Artillery lifts 100 yards.

4.30 A.M. Field guns in our front trenches cease fire, but Hotchkiss gun continues to fire.

4.31 A.M. Artillery lifts another 100 yards.

4.34 A.M. Artillery lifts to German 2nd position about 500 yards in rear of their front line.

OPERATION ORDER No. 52.

by

Brigadier General W.J.St.J. HARVEY.

Commanding Dehra Dun Brigade.

24th September 1915

4

1. 1. The GARHWAL and BAREILLY BRIGADES will assault at C.O. in accordance with programme issued.
Value of Zero will be communicated by wire.

2. As the assaulting Infantry go forward and vacate their assembly positions the DEHRA DUN BRIGADE will move forward and concentrate as shown on attached table.

3. 1st Seaforths will maintain touch with 58th Rifles and 2nd Gurkhas will maintain touch with 39th Garhwalis and will keep G.O.C. informed as these troops leave their assembly positions.

4. In the event of all troops of both advanced Brigades moving forward from our fire trenches, picquets of one N.C.O. and Nine men will posted every 100 yards XXXX in the fire trench. 2nd Gurkhas will find these picquets in IND.5.A. and 1st Seaforths in IND.5.B.
In the event of the Brigade making a further advance these picquets will rejoin Units.

5. Reports to M.33.c.4/5 up to time of forward concentration. Afterwards to junction COLVIN STREET and HOME COUNTIES TRENCH.

Issued at 11-55 a.m.

Major.
Bde Major Dehra Dun Brigade.

Copy 1 and 2 retained.
Copy 3 1st Seaforths
Copy 4 4th Seaforths.
Copy 5 9th Gurkhas.
Copy 6 2nd Gurkhas
Copy 7 93rd Infantry
Copy 8 Meerut Division
Copy 9 Bareilly Bde.
Copy 10 Garhwal Bde.
Copy 11. Jullunder Bde.
Copy 12 2 Coy Train.
Copy 13. 5 Trench Mortar Bty
Copy 14 C.R.A. Meerut Div
Copy 15. Bde M.G.O.
Copy 16. Bde.B.G.O.
Copy 17. Bde Sig O.
Copy 18. Bde Grenadier O.
Copy 19. 4th Bde R.F.A.
Copy 20. 13th Bde R.F.A.

UNIT.	PLACE.	HeadQuarters	ROUTE.
2nd Gurkhas.	HOME COUNTIES TRENCH, SOUTH of COLVIN STREET.	Near COLVIN STREET.	SUNKEN STREET and SOUTH TILLELOY ST.
1st Seaforths	Trench along N edge of RUE TILLELOY.	Near Junction MIN STREET & RUE TILLELOY.	NORTH TILLELOY and BIRDCAGE STREETS.
4th Seaforths	"B" LINE. ~~North~~ SOUTH of SOUTH TILLELOY STREET.	Junction LAFONE STREET and "B" LINE	SUNKEN STREET.
9th Gurkhas.	"B" LINE. North of MOATED GRANGE STREET.	Junction NORTH TILLELOY STREET and "B" LINE.	1 Coy via SOUTH TILLELOY ST (To follow Bde Machine Guns). 2 Coys via NORTH TILLELOY STREET. 1 Coy via BIRDCAGE STREET.
Grenadier Company.	HOME COUNTIES TRENCH, NORYH of COLVIN ST.	Junction COLVIN and HOME COUNTIES TRENCH	SOUTH TILLELOY STREET.
Bde Machine Guns.	HOME COUNTIES TRENCH North of COLVIN STREET	Junction COLVIN & HOME COUNTIES TRENCH	SOUTH TILLELOY ST (To follow Grenadier Company).
Bde Head Quarters	BAREILLY BDE Advanced Report Centre	Junction COLVIN STREET and HOME COUNTIES TRENCH	SOUTH TILLELOY STREET
Bde Bomb Guns.	Trench along N edge of RUE Tilleloy.	Near Junction MIN STREET and RUE TILLELOY	BIRD CAGE STREET (To follow 9th Gurkhas).

No B.M. 9.   Head Quarters Dehra Dun Brigade.

24th September 1915.

From.

The Brigade Major

Dehra Dun Brigade.

To.

The Officer Commanding

1st Seaforths.
4th Seaforths.
9th Gurkhas.
2nd Gurkhas.

I forward herewith copies of the undermentioned 1/10000 trench maps, as noted below:-

Sheet 36.S.W.1....................3 Copies.

Sheet 36 S.W.2....................[illegible] Copies.

Sheet 36. S.W3....................3 Copies.

Sheet 36.S.W.4....................[illegible] Copies.

Sheet 36.N.W.1....................1 Copy.

Sheet 36.N.W.2....................1 Copy.

Also one COPY of BELGIUM and FRANCE. SHEET 36. 1/40000

Major.

Brigade Major Dehra Dun Brigade.

"A" Form. Army Form C. 2121.

MESSAGES AND SIGNALS. No. of Message

Prefix Code m. | Words 44 | Charge | This message is on a/c of: Service. | Recd. at m.

Office of Origin and Service Instructions. | Sent At m. To By | (Signature of "Franking Officer.") | Date From By

TO { all Units

Sender's Number.	Day of Month	In reply to Number	AAA
*BM 30	25th		

rations	for	1st	seaforths	4th
seaforths	and	9th	gurkhas	will
be	opposite	B	subsection	head
quarters	on	RUE	TILLELOY	at
8.15	pm	tonight	aaa	rations
for	93rd	infantry	and	2nd
gurkhas	will	be	drawn	at
their	billets			

From
Place Dehra Dun Bde
Time

The above may be forwarded as now corrected. (Z)

Censor. Signature of Addressor or person authorised to telegraph in his name.

* This line should be erased if not required.

(632) —McC. & Co. Ltd., London.— W 11400/2045. 100,000. 2/15. Forms C 2121/10.

"A" Form. Army Form C. 2121.

MESSAGES AND SIGNALS. No. of Message

Prefix ... Code ... m.	Words 22	Charge	This message is on a/c of:	Recd. at ... m.
Office of Origin and Service Instructions.	Sent		... Service.	Date
	At ... m.			From
	To			
	By		(Signature of "Franking Officer.")	By

TO { 4th Seaforths

Sender's Number	Day of Month	In reply to Number	AAA
* BM 29	25		

dehra	dun	bde	is	to
be	ready	to	move	at
one	hours	notice	tonight	

From
Place Dehra Dun Bde
Time

The above may be forwarded as now corrected. (Z)

Censor. Signature of Addressor or person authorised to telegraph in his name.

* This line should be erased if not required.

202146--W. & S. Ltd., London.—W 14142/641—90,000—4/15. Forms C 2121/10.

"A" Form.

Army Form C. 2121

MESSAGES AND SIGNALS.

No. of Message

Prefix Code m. | Words 18 | Charge

Office of Origin and Service Instructions

Sent

At m.

To

By

This message is on a/c of:

Service.

(Signature of "Franking Officer.")

Recd. at 7 p.m.

Date 25.9.15

From

By

TO 4th Seaforths

Sender's Number	Day of Month	In reply to Number	AAA
*BM 6	25th		

concentrate in forward assembly position

[signature] Gordon

From
Place D D Bde
Time

The above may be forwarded as now corrected.

(Z)

Censor.

Signature of Addressor or person authorised to telegraph in his name

* This line should be erased if not required.

202146--W. & S. Ltd., London.—W 14142/641—90,000—4/15. Forms C 2121/10.

"A" Form. Army Form C. 2121.

MESSAGES AND SIGNALS.

No. of Message

Code m.	Words 83	Charge	This message is on a/c of:	Recd. at m.
Office of Origin and Service Instructions.	Sent		Service.	Date 2/15
	At m.			From Bohy
	To			
	By		(Signature of "Franking Officer.")	By

TO: [illegible] Seaforths / 4th Seaforths / [illegible] Gurkhas / 9th Gurkhas

Sender's Number.	Day of Month	In reply to Number	AAA
* ~~21~~ BM21	25		

brigade	will	concentrate	for	attack
as	under	aaa	2nd	gurkhas
front	and	support	line	from
SOUTH	MOATED	GRANGE	STREET	to
COLVIN	STREET	aaa	1st	seaforths
front	and	support	line	from
SOUTH	MOATED	GRANGE	STREET	to
NORTH	TILLELOY	STREET	aaa	4th
seaforths	front	and	support	line
from	COLVIN	STREET	to	SOUTH
TILLELOY	STREET	aaa	9th	gurkhas
front	and	support	line	from
NORTH	TILLELOY	STREET	to	NORTH
MOATED	GRANGE	STREET		

From
Place D D Bde
Time

The above may be forwarded as now corrected.

Censor.

(Z)

Signature of Addressor or person authorised to telegraph in his name.

* This line should be erased if not required.

(332) —McC. & Co. Ltd., London.— W 11400/2045. 100,000. 2/15. Forms C 2121/10.

Missing men have not [illegible]

[Fire Trench]
are 1 and 2 Coys ~~post~~ line

180 are 3 and 4 Coys [illegible]

are two [illegible] [illegible] ~~are~~ [illegible]

line } 1/2 1/4 Seaf[illegible]

are ~~[illegible]~~ [illegible]

position now.

Operation Order 59
by Brig Genl W. J. St. J. HARVEY.
Comdg Dehra Dun Bde

25-9-15

Ref trench map.

1. Garhwal + Bareilly Bdes have taken enemys 1st + 2nd line trenches.
The advanced troops of Bareilly Bde are reported to have reached the River LAYES about 400ʸ north of the MAUQUISSART–PIETRE road.

2. The Dehra Dun Bde will attack through the Garhwal and Bareilly Bdes and advance towards PIETRE.
The MAUQUISSART–PIETRE road gives the line of direction for the centre.
When PIETRE is reached the attack will be continued towards HAUT POMMEREAU and LA CLIQUETERIE.

3. The 1st Seaforths on the left and 2nd Gurkhas on the right will carry out the attack each battalion on a one Company front.
The 9th Gurkhas will be in Brigade Reserve behind the 1st Seaforths and 4th Seaforths in Brigade reserve behind the 2nd Gurkhas

Major
[illegible] Dehra Dun Bde

SECRET

PROGRAMME FOR RIFLE, RIFLE GRENADE AND MACHINE GUN FIRE:-

1. Machine Gun fire on the enemy's wire entanglement, his front line and positions in rear will be arranged by Brigade Machine Gun Officer.

Maximum expenditure :- 1000 rounds per day.

2. Rifle Grenades:- 25 a day to be fired by IND.S.B. on enemy's trenches and wire in range.

Fire to be principally during hours of darkness.

3. Rifle Fire:- By day - Sniping by Sentries. 1500 rounds allotted to each Subsection.

By Night - 30 men in each Subsection to fire more or less continuously with the object of preventing enemy mending his parapet or wire.

Rounds allotted:- 36000 per Subsection.

4. All Rifle Grenade and Rifle fire will be under arrangements of Subsection Commanders.

No B.M.29. Major.

30-9-1915. Brigade Major Dehra Dun Brigade.

Meerut Division

1/4th Seaforth Highlanders

For October 1915

~~46th Division~~

MEERUT.

1/4th Seaforth Highrs.

121/7493

to 26 Bde in Nov.

Oct. 1915

Vol I

Secret. 7/4th Seaforth Highrs. (T.F.)

Officer i/c
Adjutant General's office
The Base.

Herewith Diary for period from 2nd October to 31st October 1915.

3/11/15 J M Geass Lieut & Q.M.
for O.C. 7/4th Sea. Highrs. (T.F.)

Date	Summary of Events	Notes, References etc.
Oct 2nd	The C.O. and Company Commanders left early to take over part of the trenches in front of FESTUBERT just NORTH of the GIVENCHY RIDGE. The Brigade paraded at 10 am and marched to near LE HAMEL. Fields were allotted to each Battalion where dinner and tea were taken. The Battalion paraded at 5 pm and marched to the new line. "Disposition of Battalion 2 Companies in firing line, one in Support and one in Reserve". We relieved a Battalion of the 57th Brigade 19th Division (New Army). The trenches were quite good, though they showed signs of rough usage, a good deal of fighting had taken place here during the Summer. Communication to the Reserve line was excellent; a trolley line ran up to this trench and then along immediately behind for about 3/4 of a mile linking up with another line to our right. The weather was splendid and although the march was longer than what we had been accustomed to, the men were very cheery.	As we thought the winter months would be spent here, every one energetically started to make the place comfortable, a few palatial dug-outs were constructed

Date.	Summary of Events	Notes references. etc
Oct 3rd	Quite day, frequent showers of rain	
4th	- do - - do - trenches in a bad state	It was noted here that when a German Patrol was out, rifle fire went on the same but the flashes appeared to go skyward, until the patrol again return when the flashes appeared to be normal
5th	More rain and more mud.	
6th	Company relief No. 3 & 4 Coys take firing line 1 & 2 Coys come back to Support and Reserve line respectively. Weather cleared up, bright sunshine	
7th	Sun shining trenches gradually drying	
8th	do. Since coming in we have had very little strafing but today a certain share was allotted to our sector with the result that a huge shell blew in part of No 4 Company parapet smothering a dug-out that contained six men. after a deal of digging they were all safely extricated feeling little the worse from there hasty burial. Another of the same size filled in about 15 yds of a communication trench The reason for this bit of shelling was accounted for their counter attacking our new line North of Hulloch	

Date	Summary of Events	Notes, references etc
Oct 9th	Companies changed over weather Good	
10th	Nothing of importance " "	
11th	— do — " "	
12th	— do — Companies changed over	
13th	The 1st Army attacked SOUTH of the LA BASSEE CANAL, a Smoke demonstration was carried out for a number of miles NORTH of the main objective. This attracted a good deal of fire especially from machine guns. A Big Quick bursting on top of a dug-out injured 3 officers and one man was severely wounded by rifle fire during this demonstration. According to the German War News the British attacked along the whole of their front during this day being repulsed nearly everywhere suffering severe losses	
14th	Fairly Quiet (weather still good) Relieved by 1/9th Gurkhas, went into "Brigade Reserve" in G.H.Q Line about 600 Yds behind the village of FESTUBERT	

Date	Summary Of Events	Notes ref etc
Oct 15th	320 Of a Carrying party	
" 16th	320 Of a Carrying Party	
" 17th	Church parade by Companies 160 Of a carrying party	
" 18th	Nothing of interest –	
" 19th	Heavy firing took place about 5 pm in the direction Of HULLOCH we were ordered to stand too and be ready to move at once if required. After about three hours the firing ceased, Stand Clear was ordered and a message was received stating that the German after a heavy bombardment of our trenches with Guns of all Calibres had attacked in Great Strength, they were driven Off after severe punishment, a few had entered part of our front trenches but were soon ejected by bombs.	
" 20th	Relieved by 10th Worcesters, Marched to billets near LA COUTURE	

Date	Summary of Events	Note ref. &c
Oct. 21st	The Battalion relieved ½ of the H.L.I. and ½ 1st Gurkhas in the trenches in front of RUE DU BOIS about 500 yds S of the ESTAIRES LA BASSEE ROAD. With the exception of No 3 Company which garrisoned two Keeps the remainder of the Battalion was in the front line each company finding own supports. The trenches were bad and in some parts so low that one had to almost creep along. The Hun was very aggressive and sniped continually, our men had grown careless after being accustomed to trenches which gave excellent cover and a certain amount of freedom behind the front parapet. Rain fell immediately after the relief was completed and kept up for the greater part of the night.	Trench Strength 430 exclusive of machine Gun section.
22nd	Intermittent shelling during the day a great deal of rifle and machine Gun fire during the night.	

Date	Summary of Events	Notes ref etc
Oct. 23rd	Our Snipers had got to work and the opposition showed signs of decreasing, a machine Gun had troubled us during the day artillery support was called for a salvo from the Guns was fired every time it spoke until it was completely silenced. This system was kept up at night with very good results. The Bosche was very talkative, and asked who we were he was answered with rifle and machine Gun fire	
" 24th	No. 2 Coy. under Lieut. C. H. Harris has done a lot of good work in building up the front parapet, parados, and traverses, using about 4,000 sandbags for this purpose, he also sent out a search party who discovered and identified a number of our men who fell on the 9th of May. Sergt Rogers who went with this party stayed rather long, the fog lifted quickly, and he was hit in the shoulder and face falling about 70 yds from our own line. Pte Robertson a stretcher bearer of No 2 Coy showed up magnificently on this occasion, he went out and dressed Rogers, rolled him into a place of safety, came back and went out again with a blanket and a drop of rum stayed with him and brought him in at dusk	

Date	Summary of Events	Notes ref etc
Oct. 24th "continued"	Pte Fraser of No 2 Coy eventually went out to Robertson's assistance	
" ~~24th~~ 29	The Battalion was relieved by the Black Watch "2nd & 4th who were linked temporary" and marched to billets between PARADIS and MERVILLE a march of over seven miles a number of men suffered with their feet after the continuous trench duty which tends to soften ones feet greatly	
" 25th	Inspection and Cleaning of Kit	
" 26	do –	
" 27	Arm drill, dressing, sizing of Companies and marching past in fours!	
" 28	The Brigade paraded for inspection by His Majesty the King; after a march of three miles in a drenching rain and a preliminary drill by the Brigadier we were all very much disappointed on the parade being dismissed without us having seen His Majesty. On this parade Lce Cpl. McRae ~~number~~ No 1 Company was presented with the Russians Order of St George 4th Class Major General JACOBS pinned the ribbon to his breast.	

Date	Summary of Events	Notes & ref. etc.
Oct. 29th	News of the King having been thrown from his horse the morning of our inspection. Rained heavily all day.	Average Strength of Battalion for month 640.
30th.	Nothing of interest. Parades under Company arrangements, Lecture to Officers by the Adjutant	17 of Draft joined from Base. Men who had been in Hospital.
31st.	Battalion Church Parade, feet inspection by the Medical Officer	

15TH DIVISION
46TH INFY BDE

1-4TH BN SEAFORTH HGDRS

1915 NOV - DEC 1915

TO 51 DIV 154 BDE.

46

15th Division

15 Div

1/4th Bn. Sea: Highrs

Nov

vol. II

K

from Meerut Div Nov 15th

Temporarily attached to 139th Bde from 7th Nov. Joined 46 Bde 16.11.15.

121

7721

Nov - Dec 1916

Nov 15

Date	Summary of Events	Ref's - Notes - Etc.
Nov. 1st	Very heavy rain during most of the day. A lecture was given by the Grenade Sergt. to Companies on the composition and method of throwing hand grenades.	
Nov. 2nd.	Battalion relieved the 39th Garwhal Rifles in reserve billets in Rue des Chavattes. The heavy rain continues, and accomodation for the men is very scanty.	
Nov. 3rd.	Still raining and foot conditions worse than ever.	
Nov. 4th	Battalion marched to Vielle Chapelle for an inspection by General Jacobs (comdg. Meerut Division) on the occasion of our leaving the Indian Army Corps. After complimenting the Batn. on its work in the Field, and its appearance on that day, he said Farewell, and expressed	

his regret that he was unable to take the Battn with him to the new theatre of war.

All ranks felt his parting words very keenly and general regret was evident at our departure from the Dehra Dun Bgde.

Nov 5th

Battalion relieved the 1/9th Gurkhas in the trenches (Square S15·d·9·6) being our right with a frontage of about 500 yards. The trenches were in a very bad condition, after the heavy rains, and owing to the mud & water, it was impossible to garrison the whole of the Line. No 3 Coy, in the Fire Line, was divided into 9 groups with 6 machine guns. Disposition of the rest of the Battn was No 4. in support in Old British trench. No 2. in the Rue du Bois & No 1 in reserve on the Rue des Berceaux. On our right were the 93rd Burmas & on our left the 39th

Punjabis. Reliefs are arranged, for Companies only doing 24 hours in the Fire trench. This method allows a Coy. after completion of its Fire trench period, to return to reserve direct, where they have opportunities of drying clothing etc.

Nov. 6th / From to-day we have been attached to the 137th Bde. 46th Nth Midland Division (T.F.), but temporarily attached to the 139th Bde which is taking over the Line held by the Bareilly & Dehra Dun Bde's. On our right were the 5th Sherwood Foresters & on our ~~right~~ left the 8th Sherwoods. Weather improving but trenches still in a very bad condition. Our snipers bagged a number of the enemy to-day, and theirs also were active. 2/Lt. F.A. Harrop being wounded in the arm.

Nov. 7th	The weather is improving, but conditions are still very bad. Disposition to-day. No 2. in Fire Line. No 1. support. No 3. Rue du Bois & No 4. in reserve.
Nov. 8th	Very fine day. Hostile artillery very active in rear of line, but no damage done. Battalion was relieved at night by 3rd Londons, with the exception of No I Coy who act as Local Reserve to 3rd Londons & will be under orders of O.C. 3rd Londons. Coys marched independently to Billets at X 4-cad. Very heavy rain & strong gale during the night & we were lucky to be out in Billets.
Nov 9th	Morning spent in drying & cleaning up generally. Coys marched to the Baths at Vieille Chapelle, & found

	arrangements there very poor indeed. The water allowance was exceedingly small, and at least two batches received no new underclothing.	Batt Strength to-day 22 Officers & 642 other ranks.
Nov 10th	Fine morning. A Fatigue party of 100 men was furnished and proceeded under an R.E. officer to Rue du Bois. A haversack ration was carried, as it was expected the fatigue would last all day. No 3 Coy relieved No 1 Coy as Local reserve to the 3rd Londons, & No 1 Coy took over the billets vacated by No 1 Coy.	
Nov 11th	Dull day & occasional rain. Day spent in cleaning up & resting.	
Nov 12th	Battalion relieved in Brigade reserve by 5th Batt. Leicestershire Regiment.	

about noon. Marched to rest billets near Calonne-sur-la-Lys. The route was via Vielle Chapelle, Lelokes & Parades. After the rains the roads were very heavy, but the marching was good, & we arrived at 3:30 p.m.

Nov. 13th	In Rest billets. No parades were held to-day.	
Nov. 14th	Morning bright & frosty. Church Parade was held by Companies at their respective billets	
Nov 15th	Fine weather continues. Parades, totalling 4 hours duration were held by Companies. Sections paraded similarly under their commanders.	

Nov 16th	Battalion left Calonne in Motor Lorries for Drouvin (K 10d.1.8) south of La Bassee Canal. Route was via Lillers, Chocques & Bethune, & the journey was accomplished in 4 hours. To-day we have been detached from the 137th Bde, and are now in the 46th Bde 15th Division. All the other units of this Brigade are of the New Army, and regret is felt at leaving our old sector north of the Canal. We are now in the sector, where the recent advance was made near Hulluch, & the ~~Horizontal~~ Hohenzollern Redoubt. At Drouvin the accomodation was very limited. Nos 3 & 4 Co's being under canvas.
Nov. 17th	Morning fine but frosty. Battalion was inspected at 10 AM. by Maj. Gen. McCracken commanding the 15th Divn. No speech

	was made by the General.	
Nov. 18th	Hard frost this morning. Companies held parades during the day also Coy route marches in the afternoon. A draft of 144 O.R. arrived to-day. They were inspected by the C.O. & afterwards apportioned to Companies.	
Nov 19th	Parades same as previous day. The Draft paraded under the Sergt. Major for handling of arms etc.	
Nov 20th	Fine morning. Parades as usual. A working party of 1 officer & 50 men from each Coy was furnished. They were conveyed by bus, & returned at 11 p.m.	

Nov. 21st.	Weather very cold. Baths at Noeux-les-Mines were allotted to the Battn in batches of 50. Church Parades were held - For Presbyterians in Drouvin School at 2 + 3 p.m by Rev. Murray Rodger. 46th B.F.A.. R.C's at Drouvin Church at 8.30 a.m	
Nov. 22nd.	Programme of work as usual, excepting that Coys were inspected by the C.O. Draft paraded with their Companies	
Nov 23rd.	Very cold morning. Companies had a route march in the forenoon. No work was done in the afternoon, and men made preparations for moving up to the trenches early next morning: Officers visited the trenches at our new position.	

Nov. 24th	Battalion marched off to the trenches at 7.30 a.m. and relieved the 5th Royal Berks Regt. The route was via Noeux-les-Mines, Mazingarbe & Vermelles. Rations were issued at Vermelles. Disposition. Nos. 1-2 & 3 Coys in Fire trench, & No 4 in supports. On our right were the 7th K.O.S.B. & on the left, the 4th Suffolks. Our position here is on the south face of the Hohenzollern Redoubt, and the trench in front is "Big Willie", famous as the chief communication trench for the Redoubt.	The method of trench duty in this Brigade is 2 days in trenches & 2 days in reserve. Owing to the length of the communication trenches & the flat nature of the ground rations have to be carried up by the men in sandbags. There are no dug-outs in the trenches here, and this arrangement of 2 days in, meets this contingency
Nov 25th	In the trenches, and very cold. Considerable shelling of the support line.	
Nov 26th	Cold morning & some snow. Battalion relieved by 10th Scottish Rifles in forenoon. Marched via Vermelles to billets at Sailly-La Bourse. As No T	

	reached the end of the Communication trench a shell landed in their midst, and buried 3 men. They were however all safely got out.	very well.
Nov 27th	Cold morning. A Fatigue party of 2 officers + 100 O.R. was furnished under an R.E. officer.	
Nov. 28th	Battalion relieved 10th S R. in the trenches at the same point as our last spell, Nos 2. 3 + 4 Coys being in the Fire trench + No 1 in support.	
Nov 29th	Hostile artillery very active on our front They shelled us continuously for 2 hours and we were expecting a visit from them, This did not materialise Our casualty list during the bombardment	

	was 1 man wounded, slightly	
Nov 30th	Battalion was relieved by 2 Coys 12th H.L.I. + 2 Coys 10th S.R. Moved to Billets in Vermelles where we acted as Brigade Reserve.	

15th Division

46th Bn

1/4th Seaforth Highrs.

Dec

Vol. III

Instructions regarding War Diaries and Intelligence Summaries are contained in F. S. Regs., Part II. and the Staff Manual respectively. Title pages will be prepared in manuscript.

WAR DIARY

or

~~INTELLIGENCE SUMMARY.~~

(Erase heading not required.)

Army Form C. 2118.

Place	Date	Hour	Summary of Events and Information	Remarks and references to Appendices
	1/12/16.		In Brigade Reserve at Vermelles. Enemy shelled us in the afternoon, but no damage was done. A fatigue party of 150 men, and also a burying party of 20 men was furnished by the Battalion.	
	2/12/15		The Battalion relieved 10th Scottish Rifles in trenches to the left of our former position. Nos 1 & 4 Companies being in firing line. No 2 Coy in supports, and No 3 Coy in reserve. The day was very quiet on both sides.	
	3/12/15		Heavy hostile shelling of our support and reserve lines, and bombing of our front line, which was ultimately silenced by our batteries. Trenches in a very bad condition with mud & water, and this caused the parapet in many places to subside. Much work was done in cleaning trenches and restrengthening parapets.	Batt. Fighting strength. Officers 24, O.R. 481
	4/12/15		Hostile artillery again very active, especially at night, when they gave us two "straffings", first at 8 pm and again at 10.30 pm. Our casualties on this occasion were nil. Conditions underfoot were worse than ever.	
	5/12/15		Morning quiet, but, in reply to our artillery fire, the enemy gave us a very warm time of it for an hour. Again our casualty list was nil. Considering that dug out accomodation was very poor, and that during three bombardments we suffered no casualties, it is evident that the enemy fire is very erratic, and probably due to "wind up". Enemy quiet at night, however.	
	6/12/15		The Battalion was relieved in the morning by the 12th H.L.I. and we moved to the same billets as before at Vermelles, where we acted as Brigade Reserve.	
	7/12/15		The Battalion was relieved in Brigade Reserve by the 8th A.&S. Hrs. and we proceeded to billets at Vaudricourt ( ) 200 of the Battalion were conveyed by bus from Philosophe ( ) The remainder marched off at 10 a.m. Route via Philosophe, Sailly Labourse, Verquigneul, and Verquin to Vaudricourt. Billeting accomodation was very good here.	

2353 Wt. W2544/1454 700,000 5/15 D. D. & L. A.D.S.S./Forms/C. 2118.

Instructions regarding War Diaries and Intelligence Summaries are contained in F. S. Regs., Part II. and the Staff Manual respectively. Title pages will be prepared in manuscript.

WAR DIARY
or
~~INTELLIGENCE SUMMARY.~~
(Erase heading not required.)

Army Form C. 2118.

Place	Date	Hour	Summary of Events and Information	Remarks and references to Appendices
	8/12/15		In rest Billets. Cleaning up generally and Company inspections.	
	9/12/15		The Battalion furnished 4 fatigue parties of 100 men per Coy. at various times during the day. They were conveyed by bus to Philosophe. While on the fatigue the men received very heavy shelling, but no casualties. Party returned in the evening.	
	10/12/15		Company parades. No 2 Coys at Baths at Verquin	
	11/12/15		Company parades. Opening of Library gifted by Sir Edward Ward's committee, where the men can receive the best of literature while out on rest.	Batn. Fighting strength Officers 24 O.R. 740
	12/12/15		Church Parades were held by Companies in the school-room at Vaudricourt. C of E and R.Cs at Labourse and Drouvin respectively.	
	13/12/15		To-day we moved into Corps Reserve at Burbure. Battalion marched off at 8.30 am and made a splendid march. Route was via Hesdigneul - Gosnay - Les Chartreux and Lozinghem.	
	14/12/15		A Fatigue party of 1 officer and 62 men proceeded by bus to Bethune for a weeks work under R.E. Remainder of Battalion spent the day cleaning up generally.	
	15/12/15		Companies were engaged in platoon drill. A reading room was opened for the use of the men.	
	16/12/15		Weather fine but very cold. Brig Gen. Mathuson inspected Batn. billets, and seemed highly pleased with the arrangements. In the morning the Div. Commander, Major General McCracken saw one or two of the Coys at training.	
	17/12/15		Platoon training according to Company programme.	
	18/12/15		Parades similar to previous day.	Batn. Fighting strength Officers 24 O.R. 721.

2353 Wt. W2544/1454 700,000 5/15 D. D. & L. A.D.S.S./Forms/C. 2118.

Instructions regarding War Diaries and Intelligence Summaries are contained in F. S. Regs., Part II. and the Staff Manual respectively. Title pages will be prepared in manuscript.

WAR DIARY
or
~~INTELLIGENCE SUMMARY.~~
(Erase heading not required.)

Army Form C. 2118.

Place	Date	Hour	Summary of Events and Information	Remarks and references to Appendices
	19/12/15		Battalion lined the streets of Burbure in the morning, as Field Marshal Sir John French passed through the Brigade area. Platoon drill continued in afternoon, and Church Parades were held in evening. Lt Col Cuthbert D.S.O. proceeded to England on leave, and temporary command of Battalion was taken over by Capt. W. Gordon.	
	20/12/15		Platoon drill by Companies. No 3 Coy and Battn snipers attended the Rifle range.	20th Dec. 15 — 2/Lt G Robson, 2/Lt C Y McGregor joined the Battn
	21/12/15		Company training. A Lecture was given by the Medical Officer to all Officers in the Recreation Room. No 2 Coy and M.G. at range.	
	22/12/15		Beautiful morning. Company drill continued. Lecture by Grenade Sergt to Companies on composition, and method of throwing grenades.	
	23/12/15		Company training as usual. Lieut Harris gave a lecture on indication & recognition of targets. A dry canteen was opened in the Girls school for the use of the Battalion.	23rd Dec 15 — Lt A.K. Fraser joins Battn.
	24/12/15		Company training continued. A lecture was given by Medical Officer to Coys on hygiene etc. Baths at Raimbert were allotted to Battn.	
	25/12/15		Xmas day. No parades were held, but church services were held for all denominations	Battn Fighting strength: Officers 27, OR 734
	26/12/15		Church Parades in the morning. Companies had a route march in the afternoon	
	27/12/15		Company training. Brig. General Mathieson inspected No 4 Coy in all details of drill etc. He was very pleased with their work, and highly complimented them. No 1 Coy and M.G. at rifle range.	

2353 Wt. W2514/1454 700,000 5/15 D. D. & L. A.D.S.S./Forms/C. 2118.

Army Form C. 2118.

Instructions regarding War Diaries and Intelligence Summaries are contained in F. S. Regs., Part II. and the Staff Manual respectively. Title pages will be prepared in manuscript.

WAR DIARY
or
~~INTELLIGENCE SUMMARY.~~
(Erase heading not required.)

Place	Date	Hour	Summary of Events and Information	Remarks and references to Appendices
	28/12/15		Company training continued.	
	29/12/15		Lectures were given by Company Officers to the men of their Companies. Lecture also by the acting Adjutant Lt. H.A. Summers to all N.C.O's. In the afternoon a Battalion route march was held.	
	30/12/15		Company training as usual. No 4 Coy at rifle range in morning and MG in the afternoon.	
	31/12/15		Brigade Route march. Battalion marched off to starting point at 8.30am, and took up their position in the column at 9a.m. Battalion returned to Buxton at 1.30pm. A Divisional Billeting scheme was held to-day to which we sent 1 officer + 9 O.R.	31st Dec 15 2/Lt H.W. Mc[illegible] joins Batt.

2353 Wt. W2544/1454 700,000 5/15 D. D. & L. A.D.S.S./Forms/C. 2118.

Proposed facilities to enable soldiers of the [illegible]

Expeditionary Force to invest in the War Loan [illegible]

oooooooooooooooooooo

1. A special Army Form (specimen attached) would be [illegible] for each individual investing money.

2. Any soldier applying to his 'Paying Officer' with a view to taking up War Loan must produce his pay book (Army Book [illegible]) for examination. The officer will then satisfy himself [illegible] that the man has sufficient credit tomeet the investment.

3. The Paying Officer will record the amount of the inves[illegible] in the Pay Book in the usual manner. The amount to be sh[illegible] in 'sterling' and described as War Loan.

4. Investments can only be accepted in multiples of Five pounds. Each £5 Stock purchased will be entered in pay bo[illegible] as 'War Loan £4. 19. 4'.

5. Special Army Form (upper portion) will then be complet[illegible] signed by the man and the Paying Officer, and forwarded to the Paymaster i/c Clearing House, Base, who, after seeing th[illegible] voucher in order, will pass it to Regimental Paymaster, Fix[illegible] Centre, dealing with the soldier's accounts.

6. The Fixed Centre Paymaster will charge the soldier's pa[illegible] account in the Active Service Ledger, sign and complete the lower portion of Special Army Form, and forward it to the War Office (or other Office connected with the issue of Stock without delay. The Paymaster, Fixed Centre, will retain the upper portion of Special Army Form as a voucher to his account.

7. The Stock certificate for amount of investment should be forwarded for safe custody to Officer i/c Records of the Regiment, for retention with the soldier's documents. The soldier is at liberty at any time to request that the Stock certificate be forwarded to any person that he may nominate. This request should be signed by the man and forwarded to the Officer i/c Records through his Commanding Officer.

8. On receipt of Stock certificate, the Officer i/c Records will notify the fact to the soldier concerned.

o o o o

www.ingramcontent.com/pod-product-compliance
Lightning Source LLC
Chambersburg PA
CBHW082008220426
43670CB00014B/2581
* 9 7 8 1 4 7 4 5 3 5 1 8 2 *